"Lisa Mangum has managed to distill a lifetime of writing wisdom into these pages. Every writer, at any stage in their career, has something profound to learn from this book."

—JENNIFER A. NIELSEN, #1 *New York Times* best-selling author

"Mangum's craft book is filled with useful tips for the novice and more tried author alike, but what really stands out is the message of hope. Mangum's words will encourage you to reach until you feel as though you can touch the sky."

—TRICIA LEVENSELLER, *New York Times* and *USA Today* best-selling author

"A worthy, must-have addition for any writer's toolkit, Lisa Mangum's *Write Fearless. Edit Smart. Get Published.* is more than a how-to book. Built for authors at all levels, this handbook delivers poignant personal experience from an author and editor about the necessary tools, mindset, and motivation for creatives to bring their ideas to the page. Lisa's stories and examples hammer home the important information in a funny, engaging tone that will make your first read fast, but this is a book you're going to want on that shelf next to your desk. It's a reference to treasure."

—KEVIN IKENBERRY, international best-selling author of *The Crossing*

"Be prepared to slay your inner demons, uplevel your next story, and launch your career! This book has the writing-success secrets you've been looking for. With her trademark heart and honesty, Mangum is a legend in this industry—and you don't want to miss her best advice!"

—ANGELA ESCHLER, CEO of Eschler Editing and best-selling author

"Craft books and books about publishing can often be dry reading, but Lisa Mangum's *Write Fearless. Edit Smart. Get Published.* is highly readable, entertaining, and full of great information. It is perfect for aspiring authors, authors preparing to find agents, and established authors who will find valuable nuggets of wisdom to add to their toolbox. It is also a breath of fresh air to read a craft book that references works of genre fiction rather than stale literary classics. This is a book I will be recommending."

—STACEY KONDLA, literary agent, The Rights Factory

"With an openness and humility that will draw you in, Lisa takes us through the creation of a novel. But not just any novel—your novel. I'll be recommending this book to all my authors before we start work together, especially the 'Edit Smart' section. This book is freakin' awesome, and if you want an inside perspective from a masterful editor with decades of XP on how to make a book work, you need to read it."

—JOSHUA ESSOE, freelance editor and author of Essoe's Guides to Writing

"A wise and witty guide for writers at every stage, I wish I'd had this years ago! This is a fantastic book for writers, like having an expert take you gently by the hand and lead you through every stage of writing and publication!"

—JESSICA DAY GEORGE, best-selling author of *Tuesdays at the Castle*

"A great guide for editors and writers alike. Lisa not only explains what you need to do to create a compelling and engaging story, but she gives examples from her own personal experience as a writer (and editor) and how she's applied it to her own work. I recommend that any author (or editor) read Lisa's book and keep it close by as a quick and easy reference."

—MIA KLEVE, MRK'd Up Editing

"When I need inspiration to write, I go to Lisa Mangum. Whether I'm reading her fiction books or asking for advice on my own craft, she is the place to go. I'm ecstatic to put her in my pocket and take her everywhere!"

—KATIE CROSS, author of *Miss Mabel's School for Girls*

"As an editor, the greatest skills Lisa brings to bear on a manuscript are a desire for clarity and the generosity of spirit needed to help the author achieve it. Both are present in abundance in this book."

—JAMES A. OWEN, author of *Drawing Out the Dragons*

"Lisa Mangum's *Write Fearless. Edit Smart. Get Published.* is an incredible tool that all unpublished authors should read! Not only does she get into the craft elements of writing, but she also digs deep and shares personal experiences that really make this book stand out!"

—LYNNETTE NOVAK, literary agent, The Seymour Agency

"There are great writers, great editors, and great teachers. Lisa Mangum is all three. *Write Fearless. Edit Smart. Get Published.* is a master class that could be taught only by someone with more than twenty years of experience in guiding countless authors through turning their stories into published works. Get. It. Now!"

—J. SCOTT SAVAGE, best-selling author of the Farworld, Mysteries of Cove, and Graysen Foxx series

Write Fearless

Edit Smart

Get Published

Other Works by Lisa Mangum

Authored Young Adult Novels

The Hourglass Door
The Golden Spiral
The Forgotten Locket
After Hello

Authored Short Stories Within Anthologies

All Hallow's Eve
The Gruff Variations
Heroic: Tales of the Extraordinary
Love Among the Thorns
Summer in New York

Edited Anthologies

One Horn to Rule Them All: A Purple Unicorn Anthology
A Game of Horns: A Red Unicorn Anthology
Dragon Writers: An Anthology
Undercurrents: An Anthology of What Lies Beneath
X Marks the Spot: An Anthology of Treasure and Theft
Hold Your Fire: Stories Celebrating the Creative Spark
Eat, Drink, and Be Wary: Satisfying Stories with a Delicious Twist
Of Wizards and Wolves: Tales of Transformation
A Bit of Luck: Alternate Histories in Honor of Eric Flint

Write Fearless

Edit Smart

Get Published

A Master Class for Fiction Writers

Lisa Mangum

Foreword by Kevin J. Anderson, #1 *New York Times* Best-Selling Author

SHADOW
MOUNTAIN
PUBLISHING

Visit us at shadowmountain.com

Library of Congress Cataloging-in-Publication Data

Names: Mangum, Lisa, author. | Anderson, Kevin J., 1962– writer of foreword.

Title: Write fearless. Edit smart. Get published. : a master class for fiction writers / Lisa Mangum ; foreword Kevin J. Anderson.

Description: Salt Lake City : Shadow Mountain, [2024] | Includes bibliographical references. | Summary: "Thousands of writers—from first-time authors to #1 New York Times best-selling authors—have learned from Lisa Mangum's masterful literary advice and inspiration. Now she's collected the best of her writing and editing tips in this helpful book that covers the entire writing and querying process, from nurturing a story idea all the way to submitting a polished manuscript"—Provided by publisher.

Identifiers: LCCN 2024017447 (print) | LCCN 2024017448 (ebook) | ISBN 9781639933013 (trade paperback) | ISBN 9781649333070 (ebook)

Subjects: LCSH: Fiction—Authorship. | Fiction—Editing. | Fiction—Publishing. | BISAC: LANGUAGE ARTS & DISCIPLINES / Writing / Fiction Writing | LANGUAGE ARTS & DISCIPLINES / Grammar & Punctuation Classification: LCC PN3355 .M27 2024 (print) | LCC PN3355 (ebook) | DDC 808.3—dc23/ eng/20240626

LC record available at https://lccn.loc.gov/2024017447

LC ebook record available at https://lccn.loc.gov/2024017448

Printed in the United States of America

Publishers Printing

10 9 8 7 6 5 4 3 2 1

To Mom and Dad.
For paper clips and photo shoots.
May it always be sunset on the Pacific Coast Highway.

The buoyant can't be held under. And I am totes buoyant.

—CUTHBERT CLARK HEMINGNOT

CONTENTS

Foreword: With Passion and Precision by Kevin J. Anderson xi

Introduction: So You Want to Write a Book 1

WRITE FEARLESS

Chapter 1: Starting the Story 11

Chapter 2: The Mathematics of Great Writing 38

Chapter 3: Voice: Making Your Manuscript Sing 79

Chapter 4: How to Write an Ending—or a Sequel—
      That Doesn't Disappoint 92

Chapter 5: Breaking Through Writer's Block 110

EDIT SMART

Chapter 6: Editing: Hang on to Your Hats and Glasses! 119

Chapter 7: A Fistful of Commas 134

GET PUBLISHED

Chapter 8: Submissions and the Slush Pile 155

Chapter 9: Query Letters and Pitching 176

Chapter 10: Quit. But If You Can't 194

Acknowledgments 209

Recommended Resources 211

Notes 215

With Passion and Precision

BookExpo America (BEA) was the largest book and publishing conference in the country—like the Super Bowl for writers. I went to it several times, and in 2012, I was brought in by my publisher ECW Press to promote the release of *Clockwork Angels*, my steampunk fantasy adventure written with legendary Rush drummer, Neil Peart.

One of the events was a big public book signing with two other authors, and I found myself sitting between Dan Wells—promoting a book titled *I Am Not a Serial Killer*—and a woman I had never met before, friendly but a little shy, whose book was a young adult romance called *After Hello*. So who was I going to talk to? Someone who loudly but unconvincingly claimed not to be a serial killer or Lisa Mangum?

We hit it off immediately—so much so that only a few hours later, we had lunch with her equally delightful husband, Tracy. We were openly weeping as we told stories about the impact that special fans had had on us. Because my book was a collaboration with Neil Peart, Tracy wasted no time telling me all his Rush fan stories and how their music had saved him during a very dark time. More tears. How could this not lead to a fast friendship?

Later, I got to know Lisa much better in her position as a professional editor at Shadow Mountain Publishing when I invited her to be a guest speaker at our annual Superstars Writing Seminar in

Colorado Springs. That was where I saw Lisa truly shine. She immediately fit in as part of "the Tribe," and her editorial savvy as well as her caring and generous spirit became apparent to all.

Representing Shadow Mountain, Lisa took countless pitches from the eager and talented writers attending Superstars. Because Shadow Mountain had very particular needs, chances weren't high that any of the pitched books would be requested.

But that didn't matter. That wasn't the point.

Lisa would listen to the ideas, help shape them, and offer encouragement (and for many of these authors, it was the first time a true professional had ever done so). Hearing only a brief description, she could nail down the weak points and also isolate the strongest parts. She could help the author do course corrections, and even though they didn't sell the book they pitched, they came away feeling inspired and convinced of how to make their project better.

But Lisa did something else too. Normally in a pitch session, the long-suffering editor tries to feign interest as one author after another attempts to sell the greatest book ever written (it rarely is). Newer authors usually aren't good at "getting to the point," homing in on what is special and unique about their novel—the so-called "elevator pitch," or log line—how to hook an editor or potential reader in a sentence or two.

Lisa's pitch sessions were also coaching sessions. She took time to help the authors practice and to become more comfortable pitching their works, directing them on what a potential editor would be looking for and what would be a turn-off. Pitching to Lisa became a rite of passage for many Superstars members.

We all quickly adopted her, and Lisa adopted Superstars right back.

In her first year, Superstars founded a memorial scholarship for one of our beloved lost members. Lisa immediately suggested that we do a fundraising anthology, and she picked up on one of the memorable lessons that my wife, Rebecca Moesta, and I teach at writing conferences: do your best work *always*, no matter the venue. "Even if you're asked to write a story for a silly Purple Unicorn anthology, make sure you write the absolute best Purple Unicorn story possible."

So, Lisa proposed we do a Purple Unicorn anthology, and she volunteered to edit it. For free. My own WordFire Press would publish it, with all profits going into the scholarship fund.

That anthology, *One Horn to Rule Them All*, did well enough that she volunteered to do a Red Unicorn anthology the following year, *A Game of Horns*. And then *Dragon Writers, Undercurrents, X Marks the Spot, Hold Your Fire,* and *Eat, Drink, and Be Wary.*

Then tragedy struck Superstars when we lost David Farland, one of our founding members, and Lisa insisted on doing a memorial anthology for Dave, *Of Wizards and Wolves*. The following year, we lost another Founder, Eric Flint, which meant Lisa shepherded yet another anthology, *A Bit of Luck*. (That's quite enough memorial anthologies for now!)

Not only is Lisa a talented editor and writer, but she is also a great friend. As an editor, Lisa is kind and generous, completely engaged, and passionate about her work. She knows how to see both the big picture and the fine details. You'll learn a lot from this book, and you'll certainly enjoy the ride.

—KEVIN J. ANDERSON, #1 *New York Times* best-selling author

INTRODUCTION
So You Want to Write a Book

Welcome, fellow writer! It's good to see you on this path. Crafting stories is a beautiful and exciting adventure with plenty of other storytellers to keep you company. I love the willingness of the storytelling community to reach out a hand and help each other, so while there might be a few bumps and maybe a detour or two along the way, know that you do not walk alone.

A couple of quick notes before we begin: While I hope you find support and advice in these pages, this book is not intended to be definitive, exhaustive, or all-encompassing. Instead, I hope it provides an introduction to a wide variety of topics related to writing, editing, and publishing. I hope it gives you some practical tools that you can apply to your own manuscript and some questions to ask yourself that might help you look at your story with fresh eyes.

As with any book about writing, take what works for you and your story and feel free to leave the rest behind. If you are still looking for guidance on a specific part of writing or editing after you finish this book, the Recommended Resources list I've included at the back of the book offers many additional titles to explore.

I know you have a story of your own to tell, and I can't wait to hear it. I hope you don't mind if I start with a story of my own.

MY ORIGIN STORY

Every protagonist has a backstory. Here's mine:

Once upon a time, there was a little girl who loved to read. She read *Mouse Soup*, and how "[Olly's] room [was] an awful mess."[1] And when she was still really young—maybe four or five years old—she took a copy of *The Secret Garden* to her mom and said, "Read this to me." So, her mom sat with the little girl in a big, green rocking chair and read to her the story of Mary and Colin and Dickon.

Of gardens and growing.

Of healing and joy.

Perhaps, then, it is no surprise that the little girl grew up with an abiding love of words and a strong respect for the power of stories and the people who tell them.

THE STORY BUSINESS

I love books. I always have. Books are my comfort and my safety. They are my reward and my escape.

Two quick stories to illustrate the kind of reader I was as a child:

When I was in elementary school, I volunteered to help in the library instead of going outside for recess. I still remember the feeling I had when, one day, I returned a book to the school library only to discover I had never checked it out in the first place. I had simply gone to the library, taken the book, and wandered back to my desk. I was mortified. I had *stolen* a book from the library! Never mind that I had returned it on time and in perfect condition; it was the principle of the thing.

Story number two: In middle school, I'd go with my mom to parent-teacher conference. I would browse the book fair in the cafeteria while she listened to all my teachers heap praise and gold stars upon my name.

Then, when Mom came to fetch me, it was easy to say, "Since I've been such a good student, will you buy these books for me?" I always went home with a stack of seven or eight books in my hands—which would last about, oh, seven or eight days.

Mom loved books as much as I did. She was a writer who wrote cookbooks and biographies and developed board games and card games, so I grew up knowing that *writing* was a Thing People Did, a job that maybe I could do one day as well. So, I wrote all the time—short stories, fragments of novels, really bad poetry—because I knew, I just *knew* that I'd write a book someday.

My mother shared her love of words and her incredible drive for creativity with me. She taught me how to build strong character relationships, how to plot a book from start to finish, and how to weave symbolism into a story. She taught me about dialogue and how powerful language could be. She taught me the proofreading marks and how to use them. She reminded me to pay attention to every single character and letter and word on the page—as well as to what was *not* on the page but should be.

I would read books aloud to her while she made cookies or crocheted afghans, and we would have long conversations about the benefits, beauty, and unparalleled practicality of paper clips.

It was my mother who would tell me, "This is great!" or, "This needs work." Most often, though, she would tell me firmly and without hesitation, "You can do it!"

And I believed her with my whole heart and soul—

All the way up until eighth grade, when I had an assignment to write my autobiography, and I wrote this: "I've tried my hand at painting and writing and frankly, the first time was the charm. My painting was pretty good for a fifth grader and writing, well I only have a few works that I'm really proud of. 'Follow Your Dreams' is the only one. I have a lot of ideas for stories, but I wasn't born with the talent for writing, so my ideas will just stay ideas."

Somehow, I had stopped listening to my mother's voice and had started listening to the voice of self-doubt in the back of my head that said, "You *can't* do it. You *shouldn't* do it. Don't you dare even *try*."

I thought I didn't have the talent to be a writer.

I thought I wasn't allowed to share my stories or my voice.

From then on, I believed that writing was a Thing *Other* People Did. Not something I could do.

THE EDITING BUSINESS

But my mom was also an editor, so I grew up knowing that *editing* was a Thing People Did, a job that maybe I could do one day as well. If I couldn't be a writer, maybe I could still do something else that my mom did. One way or another, I wanted to be in the word business—the story business.

I began working in publishing in 1997—a career currently comprising more than 25 years, more than 720 books edited, and at least 35,000 rejection letters sent—but my editing journey actually started in 1992. That was the year I began to make plans to go to college, and my mom encouraged me to write to some book editors for advice, which I did. I wrote to lots of editors, asking which classes I should take in college if I wanted to someday do what they did.

I received several replies. Some helpful, others less so, but the one that stood out to me was from Madeleine Robins at TOR. She wrote me a detailed, two-page letter filled with advice and encouragement and warnings, and it was her letter, in part, that helped me believe I could have a future in editing at a publishing house.

I graduated from the University of Utah in 1997 with a bachelor's degree in English, and I immediately applied to be the children's book buyer for a local publishing house, Deseret Book. I had worked at Waldenbooks to put myself through college, and while

I didn't have all the required experience that being a book buyer called for, I thought it might be a "fake it until you make it" situation. Secretly, I hoped that if I got the job, maybe I could wiggle my way over to production and the editorial team, which is where I really wanted to be.

I applied for the job—and I didn't get it.

Shortly after, however, I got a phone call from Deseret Book's production manager, Anne Sheffield, who said, "We got your application, and we'd like to invite you to work in the production department as one of our freelance proofreaders." (I guess my plan worked after all.)

I took the proofreading test—grammar, spelling, punctuation, plus some cold proofreading and copy-to-copy proofreading work—and got the highest score anyone had ever earned on the test. Just one month after I graduated from college, I was working in my chosen field, albeit on a freelance basis.

A few months later, my mom, who was the assistant managing editor for a national magazine, called me and said, "Keep an eye on Bookcraft Publishers. They are going to have an opening in the editorial department. I know because we are hiring one of their editors to come work for us."

When Bookcraft posted an opening for an assistant editor, I dutifully applied. I took their proofreading test. And got the highest score they had seen on that test.

And I didn't get the job.

Shortly after, however, I got a phone call from Bookcraft's editorial manager, Cory Maxwell, saying, "We would like you to come in for an interview for an editorial assistant position." (I learned later that the company essentially created an entry-level position in order to hire me.)

Four months after my college graduation, I was working full time as an editorial assistant at a publishing house. Two years later, in 1999, Deseret Book Company acquired Bookcraft, and I've been at Deseret Book Company ever since. In 2014, Chris Schoebinger asked me to be managing editor of Shadow Mountain, the national imprint of Deseret Book, which I immediately accepted.

Oh, and along the way, I discovered something amazing. It turned out that writing was a Thing I Could Do after all, and I was able to write and publish four best-selling and award-winning young adult novels. (See page 132 to learn how I got myself back into writing.)

Being an editor is a wildly exciting profession. Exhausting? Yes. Stressful? Sure. But at its core, it's all about reading books and helping them shine as brightly as they can. It is a dream job for me.

YOUR ORIGIN STORY

You might have a similar dream of becoming a writer or maybe even an editor. Perhaps you already have turned your eyes toward the possibility of publication. I'm excited to share my editing expertise and writing experience to help show you how to make your writing the best it can be.

If you are just starting out, staring at that first blank page and wondering how to even begin, there are chapters in this book that can help you find and develop your ideas. There are sections devoted to developing characters and showing you how to use those character relationships to generate conflict. There are helpful guideposts to direct you toward the climactic summit of your story, and there are encouraging stories and suggestions to empower you to break through the obstacles that might stand in your way.

When you are ready to turn to editing, you'll find my best advice for how to tackle developmental edits and revisions as well as how to become a master of punctuation and corral those pesky commas into place.

Then we'll turn our attention to writing query letters and to tips for pitching your book to an agent, editor, or publisher.

Before we embark on this journey together, I want you to take a minute to think about some important questions:

What's *your* origin story? Where did *your* dream begin? What does it look like? What does it feel like inside you?

Maybe your dream is to be published or to finish a manuscript or to learn a new skill. Whatever it is, visualize it. Hold it in your mind and in your heart. Write it down in as much detail as you can. Got it?

Good.

Let's get started.

Write Fearless

Chapter 1
Starting the Story

Beginnings are hard.

They require a supreme act of creation, bringing something into existence that has never existed before, and that takes effort, intention, and energy.

If you're like me when it comes to creating a story, you sometimes suffer from the paralysis of perfection—the idea that the very next page, paragraph, sentence, or word must be perfect, or else your novel will automatically be a failure. Plus, you've read loads of amazing books in your lifetime. How could your book possibly stack up when compared to those? What made you think you could write a book at all?

If the sight of a blank page inspires panic, remember to embrace your ability to enact change. You have the power to change that blank page into one with words, and best of all, those words don't need to be great, and they certainly don't need to be perfect; the words just need to be there. Step one of writing a book is simply to write all the words.

Easier said than done, I know. (If you want to jump ahead to chapter five on breaking through writer's block, go ahead.)

STRIVE TO WRITE FEARLESS

Wait! Don't put the book down! I know it seems like a tall order to "write fearless" when you might already feel a great deal of fear about trying to write your story at all. If it helps, think of the word in two parts—*fear less*. It's normal to be unsure or apprehensive or even downright terrified at the beginning of this process. Strive to fear *less* every time you sit down to work on your story.

Fear *less* about what other people might say about your work. (Or even what *you* might say to yourself about your work.)

Fear *less* when it's time to tackle revisions or learn how to properly use a semicolon.

Fear *less* when you have the chance to follow a character into the unknown wilderness of their backstory—even if it means leaving behind your outline for a time.

After some practice of fearing *less*, you will be ready to write *fearless*.

Story Time with Lisa

It was January 2018, and I was having a hard time. My cat Allie had just died. She was seventeen years old, which is pretty old for a cat, but her death was totally unexpected.

I had noticed she wasn't feeling great. She was a little sluggish, and she was a lot more snuggly than usual. So, one morning, I took her to the vet, and to help keep her calm on the way, I told her about an upcoming convention I was going to for the TV show *Supernatural*. The cast would be taking pictures and signing autographs, and I really wanted to have a photo with the three leads of the show. But the photo was expensive, and I was afraid it would be out of my budget.

Once we got to the vet's, I turned all my attention to helping Allie. The vet got us right in, and I was sure they would give Allie a boost, maybe change her diet, and send us home. Instead, the vet said Allie had advanced kidney disease, and we would need to let her go that very day.

About a week after I said goodbye to Allie, my friend Gina invited me to a writing retreat with some other friends. She challenged me to write 10,000 words over the weekend. I nearly laughed. I was still grieving; I was having a hard enough time getting through the days—forget trying to be creative. Besides, the most words I had ever written in a weekend was just shy of five thousand, so ten felt impossible. But I told myself that if I did reach that goal, I'd buy myself that photo op I had told Allie about.

During that weekend, any time I started to lag or feel myself stall or fear that the story wasn't going anywhere, I would think about Allie and our last day together. I'd think about the photo I wanted, and I would say, "Just write the words, Lisa, even if they're not great." The goal was not to write 10,000 great words; it was to write 10,000 words.

Pretty soon, I found a rhythm to my work. Yet inevitably, I would feel that same creeping fear returning, and whenever it did, I would pause, take a breath, summon my courage, and write *one more word*.

I wrote more than 10,000 words that weekend, and I got my photo. When I look at it, I remember Allie, and I remember that weekend, and I remember that it is possible to do hard things if you give yourself grace and follow your courage past your fear.

When I find myself feeling nervous, afraid, or overwhelmed, I give myself permission to write a bad first draft. I even challenge myself to write the draftiest first draft I can, because I know shaping and polishing and perfection can come later. A first draft simply needs to *exist* before you can do anything with it.

I love this quote from Shannon Hale: "When writing a first draft, I have to remind myself constantly that I'm only shoveling sand into a box so later I can build castles."[1]

Don't panic when your first draft doesn't look like a castle at the start. But as with undertaking any building project, you'll want to gather some supplies first:

- an idea
- a plot structure
- a point of view
- a writing process

I HAVE AN IDEA!

"Where do you get your ideas?" I usually hear that question from beginner writers who are still trying to figure out their place in the flow of creativity. The truth is, ideas are cheap and easy and everywhere. They're not all automatically *good* ideas, so part of your job as a writer is to learn how to identify and parse out the best ideas and then combine them in ways that haven't been done before.

If you are having a hard time trying to decide whether the idea you are nurturing is good or bad, ask yourself two questions: first, "Have I seen this idea done before?" It's okay if the answer is yes. Lots of stories are born from similar ideas.

The second question to ask is, "Am I excited enough about this idea to do what it takes to make it my own?" The seed of your idea will need to go through rigorous development as you help it grow throughout your story. You'll need to push it to its limits, pull it into a new shape, maybe even hack off a chunk that doesn't seem to be going anywhere. All that will take time and effort, but if you are truly excited about the idea and committed to it, chances are high that you can make nearly any idea work for your story.

Story Time with Lisa

Early on in my book tour for *The Hourglass Door*, I was spending the day talking to students at a middle school. It was lunchtime,

14

and I was sitting in the cafeteria with the teachers. A couple of tables down from us, I saw a young boy sitting alone with a slice of pepperoni pizza on his plate. I watched as he methodically and deliberately took every single pepperoni slice off his pizza and replaced them with slices of dill pickles, one after the other. I had never seen such a thing.

He caught me watching him, and he grinned and said, "It's so good," and he took a huge bite.

I thought, *Oh, no, it couldn't be.*

But the image stayed with me, in part because while I've heard of pineapple on pizza, I've never heard of pickles on pizza, and I realized that could be the seed of an interesting idea.

What if this little boy loved pickles on pizza because he actually wasn't from this planet and he couldn't digest pepperoni, but he could digest the vinegar and acidity of pickles? What kind of story could be built around a boy who has come to Earth for the first time and is trying to figure out what to eat and how to survive?

Be observant; look for the strange and unusual happenings in the world, because you'll never know when a spark will inspire a new story.

Feed Your Brain

Another way to help fill your idea bucket is by staying curious. Did you know scientists have learned how to erase memories out of rats' brains?[2] Did you know a fungus can transform ants into zombies?[3] Did you know bananas are radioactive?[4]

Most writers love to read fiction, but how many of us browse the nonfiction shelves of the bookstore, looking for education and inspiration? Learning about science and technology, history and biology, society and art, music and politics can feed our brains and increase our creativity.

Stay connected to your creativity. That may not always be writing every day. Your creativity may flourish by doing a paint night at the library, going to the movies, or working on a jigsaw puzzle while you're watching TV. Maybe you'd like to learn how to make pottery or write a song.

I once read an article called "This Is Your Brain on Jane Austen." Researchers took brain scans of people who were reading textbooks or other material that required a certain type of focus and concentration, and then they did similar scans of people who were given Jane Austen to read just for fun, just for pleasure, and to everyone's surprise, different areas of the subjects' brains lit up.[5]

When your creative brain is feeling taxed, when you are drained from intense focus and concentration, put down your own work and pick up somebody else's. Enjoy the simple pleasure of reading a story for fun, and activate and feed another part of your brain.

A side benefit of reading for fun within the genre you write is that it can help you identify the tropes that work, the formulas that exist, and the themes and trends in the marketplace. Reading outside the genre you traditionally write in can also help deepen your knowledge of tropes and formulas that perhaps you haven't experimented with yet. A romance writer who reads mysteries could then be well-positioned to write a romantic suspense. A contemporary YA author who reads epic fantasy may pick up some helpful pointers on world-building.

When we stay curious, observant, and hungry for new information, ideas become easier to find. Once we find them, though, how do we turn them into stories?

One way is to keep an idea journal. Grab a notebook, or use the notes app on your phone and write down five things every day that you find interesting or engaging. It could be something you see or overhear or even smell. Then pick one of those ideas and write five wildly different what-if scenarios using that experience as a springboard. This exercise is a great way to help develop and strengthen creativity as well as help overcome the natural inclination to reject an idea because it's "silly."

All ideas have potential. It's up to you to identify the ideas that resonate with you—the ideas that want to be written—and then bring the best ones to life.

PICK A PLOT

Plot is simply how you get your characters from point A to point B, from chapter one to the epilogue. There are numerous ways to accomplish that, just as there are lots of different ways you can travel from Los Angeles to New York. You could go by foot—it would take a long time, but you could do it—or you could take a plane or a train or a car or a zeppelin or a boat or even a riding lawnmower. Some paths might be more straightforward, while others might take a more circuitous route.

When it comes to plot structure, there are plenty of paths to choose from. Here are just a few:

- **The Hero's Journey:** This is the classic structure Joseph Campbell developed in his book *The Hero with a Thousand Faces.* There are seventeen steps to this cycle, but at the core, it "involve[s] a hero who goes on an adventure, is victorious in a decisive crisis, and comes home changed or transformed."[6] Matthew Winkler and Kirill Yeretsky also created an excellent video summary of this structure, which is available on YouTube.[7]
- **The three-act structure:** "Act one: exposition, inciting action, turning point into act two; Act two: rising action, midpoint, turning point into act three (often a 'dark night of the soul'); Act three: pre-climax, climax, denouement."[8]
- **The seven-point arc:** This method breaks down the structure into seven steps rather than three acts. The steps are

the hook, plot point 1 (inciting incident), pinch point 1 (antagonist introduced), midpoint, pinch point 2 (obstacles increase), plot point 2 (climax), and resolution.[9]

- **The snowflake method:** This process starts small, with a one-sentence summary of your book, and then you add more and more elements to the core idea until you have "three disasters plus an ending."[10]

- **Scene and sequel:** The "scene" covers the action the character undertakes in order to achieve a goal, while the "sequel" gives the character time to react to what has happened—both emotionally and logically—and to consider their options and then make choices that will lead to a new goal, which will require new action.[11]

- *Save the Cat!*: Originally developed for screenplays, this formula contains a list of fifteen story beats (or plot points) that draws upon structural elements of both the Hero's Journey and the three-act structure to create a story that corresponds to the pacing of a traditional Hollywood movie.[12]

Whole books have been written about each one of them; I have included many of those books in the Recommended Resources at the end of this book. (One of the best is *The Mercenary Guide to Story Structure* by Kevin Ikenberry.[13])

We'll talk about several plot structures throughout this book, but in the end, it almost doesn't matter which method you choose.

The goal for your structure is the same for your story: forward progression, increased momentum, and unrelenting tension.

Each plot structure brings something different to the table, and some of them work better with certain genres than others do. For example, fantasy often finds its stride in the Hero's Journey, while "Save the Cat" works well for action and adventure stories. You may find that different stories respond better to different plot structures, so if you're struggling to chart a path through your story, be fearless enough—and flexible enough—to try a new method to see if that brings clarity to your process.

While your plot structures your story, *plot* and *story* maintain important differences. Plot essentially tells *what* the events that happen are. You can graph them on a chart, from the inciting incident through the rising action to the climax, then through the falling action to the resolution. Or you can create an outline of point-by-point moments that get you from point A to point B.

But story helps *show* the evolution. It explains *why* the events are happening. It also helps fill in the gaps between the plot points on your chart. Those gaps are where the story lives and breathes and captures our imagination.

Story Time with Lisa

When I was writing *The Hourglass Door*, I started with a detailed outline. I made a list of "This is what happens in chapter one, and this is what happens in chapter two," all the way through the thirty chapters I had planned. I wrote the first three chapters, and then I wrote the last three chapters, and then I jumped around and wrote whatever scenes I felt like.

It didn't take long before I realized my outline no longer resembled the story I was writing, but I didn't mind because I was having fun discovering the plot with these characters, who were coming to life the more I wrote about them. When I finished writing all the scenes that I could think of, I stitched the book together—all 100,000 words of it—and I thought, "Oh my goodness, I have written a book."

When it came time to write book two, *The Golden Spiral*, I thought, "I know how to do this. I'll work up an outline, then I'll write the first three chapters and the last three chapters, and then I'll just write everything in between."

That didn't work.

My outline was a mess from the start because I couldn't see far enough down the path to even know the shape of the story or what the characters were going to do. I struggled to make sense of what little I did know.

Eventually, I bought a stack of colored index cards, assigned one color to each character, then cut the cards into little squares. I wrote down all the important scenes I knew I would need in the book—like the First Kiss, an Argument That Leads to a Revelation, and a Surprise! Plot Twist!—based on which character would be most prominent in the chapter.

Then I sat on the floor and dealt the cards out, chapter by chapter. What needed to happen in chapter one? What needed to happen in chapter two?

The bird's-eye view allowed me to put my arms around the story in a different way, and I moved those little cards around until I was sure I had a good flow of purple cards and yellow cards and blue cards and that I had the right number of scenes with my protagonist, the love interest, and the antagonist.

There are several writing programs, including Plottr and Scrivener, that offer a similar kind of brainstorming format with corkboards and cards that you can move around, or you could simply hang a large whiteboard on a wall and use it to break down the story into smaller sections to tackle. For me, it was satisfying to physically shuffle the story-point cards and make order out of chaos.

Once I felt good about the flow, I gathered the cards in order, and starting with page one, chapter one, paragraph one, word one, I wrote the book one scene after another, straight through, from beginning to end.

When it was time to write book three, I thought, "*Now* I know how to write a book." I got my trusty little index cards out, I sat on the floor, and . . . it did not work.

Writing book three was not a delightful frolic with friendly characters, nor was it following a shopping list of scenes. It felt more like hacking through a dense jungle with a dull machete. The only way to get to the end was to do the work and power through it, one word at a time.

After I'd written the first half of the book and realized I didn't have any idea how the story was going to end, I sat down and wrote nearly five thousand words, stream-of-consciousness style, of everything I knew about the story and where I wanted it to go. I didn't try to block it out into scenes or chapters. I just threw a lifeline out into the dark and followed where it led.

Don't be afraid to listen to your story and find the plotting path that works best for you.

A POINT OF VIEW

Just as different plot structures might work better for different stories, the same holds true for choosing a point of view (POV).

There are pros and cons to each narrative style—first, second, or third person—and you'll also want to consider both the age group of your audience and the genre to decide which one you want to use for your story.

Quick terminology definition: When we talk about a *narrator*, that simply means "the perspective the story is told from." That means the "narrative voice" of your story is often (but not always) also your "character voice." (We'll talk more about character voice in chapter three.)

Here is a quick summary of each POV style.

First Person

First person draws the reader deep into the mind and heart of your main character. We see and experience the world through their eyes. It often feels easy and natural to write from this POV, and being limited to that single viewpoint can help create a strong voice for your character.

- I heard the waves crashing on the shore as I fell asleep.
- Kevin frowned, and I knew he was mad that I'd eaten the last cookie.

One drawback of first-person POV is that because you are staying in a single perspective, you can't jump into another part of the narrative unless your character is participating in the action. It also means you have to rely on body language and dialogue for your POV character to know what other characters are thinking and feeling.

It is possible to write a book with several characters all using a first-person POV, but in those cases, it can be helpful to indicate the character's name whenever a switch is made.

Second Person

Second-person POV means the author or character is addressing the reader directly. (Remember the Choose Your Own Adventure series? It's like that.)

- You listen to the waves crashing on the shore as you fall asleep.
- "You ate the last cookie without telling me?" (This type of usage also works well in dialogue, obviously.)

Occasionally, in a first-person POV story, the character may have an internal thought or make an observation that breaks the fourth wall and uses the pronoun *you* in referring to the reader. That's different from writing an entire book in second person, which is rarely done and difficult to master. However, two books that skillfully utilize second-person POV are *The Night Circus* by Erin Morgenstern and *All the Truth That Is in Me* by Julie Berry.

Third Person, Omniscient

Third-person POV can be either omniscient or limited, and the omniscient style allows the viewpoint to travel between all the characters all the time.

While third-person omniscient was once a more popular point-of-view choice—*Dune* by Frank Herbert was written in that style—its current usage is considered by many readers, reviewers, and editors to be a mistake or a sign of an amateur writer. You can still write in this POV; just be aware of the risks.

- Charlie listened to the waves crashing on the shore. She loved falling asleep to the sound. (third-person limited)
- Kevin frowned, mad that Charlie had eaten the last cookie. She felt guilty and wondered how she could make it up to him. (third-person omniscient) We are in Kevin's POV, which is how we know he is mad, but then we "head hop" into Charlie's POV to learn that she feels guilty.

"Head hopping" and fracturing the viewpoint between multiple characters at any given time not only runs the risk of your reader becoming lost as to which character they are supposed to follow but also risks that the reader might not might not connect with the characters on a deep, emotional level.

Also, if you switch point-of-view characters within the same paragraph or sentence, your writing can feel choppy and clunky.

Third Person, Limited

Like first-person POV, a third-person-limited viewpoint is fixed on a single character's perspective, which allows you to concentrate on telling a strong story from a relatable character with a distinctive voice.

But unlike first person, this option gives you the ability to switch to a different character's POV at a chapter break or a section break.

This allows you to change the action or move to a different part of the story at a natural breaking point without confusing the reader.

Different genres support multiple third-person POVs better than others. For example, a sprawling epic fantasy could have eight or nine POV characters, while a romance would typically have two at the most.

When switching viewpoints, ask yourself, "Which character has the most critical piece of information that the reader needs to know right now?" The answer can help you effectively guide the story's pacing.

How Do I Choose?

Here are a few questions to ask yourself to help choose a point-of-view style:

How close do I want to be to the character?

Nancy Kress offered this helpful answer: "First person [is] a matter of intimacy. . . . Third person [is] a matter of distance. . . . Close third person POV is a lot like first person. It can have much of the individual flavor of speech, much of the intimate ruminations . . . but not all. The reader is still receiving descriptions from the outside."[14]

What do I want to accomplish?

If your character has an individual, distinctive voice, first person is probably a smart choice.

If your story will have lots of internal thoughts, again, first person is probably the way to go. It will save you from having to italicize half your book.

If you are feeling daring or avant-garde (or are writing poetry, flash fiction, or litRPG), second person might give you the tools you need to tell your story effectively.

Do you want to give the narrator an authorial voice as well? If so, choose third person.

Do you have a large cast of characters? Third person would be a good way to help your reader differentiate between everyone.

Which character has the most to lose?

The character who has the most to lose in a scene or who will grow the most over the course of the story can be a good choice for your point-of-view character because it gives you the greatest opportunity to tell the most interesting part of the story.

The Lord of the Rings by J. R. R. Tolkien is told primarily through the point of view of the hobbits, who were not warriors or kings or wizards. They did not have much power, so they provided a unique perspective on the world-changing events in Middle-earth.

Story Time with Lisa

I knew two things when I sat down to plot *After Hello.*

I knew it was going to be a stand-alone, contemporary, young adult love story with two main characters, Sam and Sara, and I knew I was going to alternate chapters between their first-person POVs.

I started chapter one from Sara's point of view, first person: "I shouldn't have noticed him. I wasn't even looking in his direction at first. I was dazzled by the sunlight reflecting off the glass buildings that lined the busy sidewalks of New York."[15]

I felt really good about the chapter, so I started chapter two with Sam's point of view. I was halfway through when I realized I had switched into third person: "Someone was following him. It was a crazy idea; there were always people walking along the narrow sidewalk, so it was impossible to believe there could be just one person intent on following him, but he knew it as surely as he knew the exact contents of his messenger bag."[16]

I paused and thought, *Do I switch him to first person, or do I finish writing this chapter in third person?* It felt right to stay in third person for Sam's point of view, so I finished the chapter.

Chapter three went back to Sara—and back to first person—and I thought, *I'm never going to be able to pull this off. Books aren't written like this.*

But it felt right and easy, so I continued that pattern back and forth—Sara and Sam, first and third—for the whole book.

I gave the manuscript to my beta readers for their feedback, and after they turned in their notes, I asked each one of them specifically, "Did the point of view switch from first to third bother you?" And they all said, "What switch?"

Even though that style was not done frequently, it worked. It didn't trip up the reader; it didn't slow down their experience. So, I left it. When I turned in the manuscript to my editor, I asked for her opinion, and she agreed that the style I had used worked for that particular story.

Not every book will be told in first and in third, but I believe your book and your characters will tell you which point of view will work best for that project.

A WRITING PROCESS

There is no one right way to write a book, but there might be a right way for *you* to write *your* book. One of the best things a writer can do is figure out what processes and practices work best for them.

One method might be to set a goal to try to write every day. You'll notice I didn't say "write every day" but "*try* to write every day." Writing is hard, and sometimes it's just not in you. Sometimes the creative well has run dry, you're tired, you're sad, or you've got too many appointments cluttering your calendar. I've been there. Just open the page and write "I tried."

Another method might be to focus on a daily word-count or a weekly page-count goal. It might work for you, but for other people, that kind of required structure could be stifling.

I've never done NaNoWriMo, where authors are challenged to write a 50,000-word novel in the month of November, but if you know you're a slow writer, setting a deadline to write 50,000 words in thirty days might cause you more stress than is beneficial. Alternatively, if you know you can draft fast, maybe that same goal isn't much of a challenge.

It's a lot—being a writer or an editor—so whenever I feel overwhelmed by the amount of work I have to do on a project, or when the finish line I want to reach feels oh-so-far away, or when that "paralysis of perfection" returns and dumps me into a writing slump, I remind myself: "Everything counts."

If you write one sentence today, great—that counts. If you write ten thousand words, great—that counts. If you write five hundred "not great" words—that counts. If your day gets completely away from you and you just think about your book for only half an hour—that counts too. (Maybe what *doesn't* always count is bingeing YouTube and thinking, "I should really be working on my book.")

The mantra Everything Counts is a way for me to remember to celebrate every milestone along the way because *all* work is valuable. And the more you work at your craft, the better you can become.

In the writing process, there are many places to start, but the reading process starts with the all-important first sentence.

THE FIRST SENTENCE

This feels like the truth:

Editors care so much about the first line of the manuscript, they will make a decision on a project based solely on that sentence.

Therefore, your first sentence must be the single greatest thing you ever write in your entire life.

Although it feels like the truth, it's probably overstating that line's importance a little.

Conversely, editors and agents really don't have that much time to spend on reviewing manuscripts, and while I wish I had time to read every submission in full, that is simply not possible. So, yes, I do make a lot of decisions based on a query letter and the first couple of pages of a manuscript.

Here are a few tips I would recommend you do—or don't do—when starting your manuscript.

Prologues

I think prologues can actually be good; three of my four published books have them. They can help set the mood or the tone of the story or even introduce the theme. But please don't use a prologue as a place to dump your backstory or insert excessive exposition.

Ask yourself, "Is this prologue strong enough to do the job of introducing the reader to the character, the story, and the world? Or should this be chapter one?"

The question whether to include a prologue depends on both the audience you are writing for and your genre. I'm not sure middle-grade readers appreciate the nuance of a finely crafted prologue. Likewise, a picture book doesn't need a prologue at all. Epic fantasy frequently employs prologues. Romance usually does not.

If you choose to write a prologue, keep it short and have a specific purpose in mind for why it needs to be in the book.

Showcase Something Special

I love reading manuscripts that showcase something special about the story on the first page. That could be anything from a heroic-character moment to posing a question that demands to be answered to introducing a memorable voice.

Author Donald Maass offered this suggestion: Find a place in the first page, maybe even the first paragraph, to give your character a moment to be heroic.

Make a list of the heroic qualities of your main character. It could include merits such as loyalty, intelligence, creativity, humor, strength, kindness, or intuition. Then pick one of those virtues and find a way to showcase it in a small way on the first page.[17]

That will do two things: First, it will help endear the character to us; we will admire that character for the heroic quality on display. Second, it will lay the groundwork for that same heroic quality to shine at the end of the story.

For example, if your protagonist demonstrates a moment of compassion in the first couple of pages of the book, when they draw upon that same heroic quality of compassion to defeat the antagonist at the end of the book, we will say, "Of course! We knew they had it in them all along. We saw it on page one."

You might also use the first page to hint at a mystery yet to come, even if you're not writing a mystery. Every story has questions that need to be answered, and the first one can be a small question, a small mystery—something that inspires curiosity in the reader to keep turning the pages.

Manuscripts stand out when they have a strong voice, either from a character or the narrator, right from the beginning. (We'll talk more about voice in chapter three.)

Ultimately, what I want to see on the first page of a manuscript is an invitation to continue reading, whatever that looks like. It could be a beautiful metaphor or some lovely description. It could be a smart turn of phrase. It could be a fast action scene. It could be witty banter.

Find the thing you are best at and showcase *that* on the first page.

Here are some examples of first lines from some of my favorite books that help show the variety of ways you can start a book.

Start with action. The opening sentence of *The Dark Tower, Volume 1: The Gunslinger* by Stephen King is a classic and one of my all-time favorites: "The man in black fled across the desert, and the gunslinger followed."[18]

Not only does this sentence introduce us to the two main characters, but it also gives us a sense of action. "The man in black fled"—he is running fast and far and with some measure of fear. "And the gunslinger followed"—but the gunslinger is not running; he's not chasing. He's *following*. The deliberate use of that verb suggests the gunslinger is determined, implacable, unrelenting, and unwavering. We will see all those qualities as we come to know the gunslinger through the course of the story, but we get a glimpse of them all here in this opening sentence.

Start with a threat. "There was a hand in the darkness, and it held a knife."—Neil Gaiman, *The Graveyard Book*.[19]

We don't know what that hand holding the knife is going to do, but we know it isn't going to be good. We feel compelled to turn the page to see what happens.

Start with a character. *The Far Pavilions* by M. M. Kaye is a 1,200-page historical novel set in 1857, which means I am already anticipating a story filled with deep descriptions and intercut plot lines and a vast cast of characters. I'm also not surprised when we begin with the birth of the main character: "Ashton Hilary Akbar Pelham-Martyn was born in a camp near the crest of a pass in the Himalayas, and subsequently christened in a patent canvas bucket."[20] Because the book is 1,200 pages long.

Start with a strong voice. *Riddley Walker* by Russell Hoban is set roughly 2,000 years after nuclear war has returned the world to a prehistoric Iron Age, and the prose is essentially written phonetically from the point of view of the twelve-year-old protagonist. I found myself needing to read it out loud to hear what I was saying so my brain could match it to what was on the page. Riddley has a very distinctive character voice: "On my naming day when I come 12 I gone front spear and kilt a wyld boar he parbly ben the las wyld pig on the Bundel Downs any how there hadnt ben none for a long time befor him nor I aint looking to see none agen."[21]

Start with an event. *Oryx and Crake* by Margaret Atwood opens with a simple sentence: "Snowman wakes before dawn."[22]

There is an oft-quoted rule about not starting a book with a character waking up, and for the most part, I agree with that. But in this case, Snowman is not waking from a dream, nor does he immediately look at himself in the mirror. He simply wakes before dawn.

Start with the setting, specifically identifying a time. Again, this is from Margaret Atwood. The first sentence of *The Blind Assassin* is "Ten days after the war ended, my sister Laura drove a car off a bridge."[23]

Start with the setting, highlighting the location. I will buy just about any book written by Tad Williams, sight unseen, and a particular favorite series is his high-tech science-fiction epic, Otherland. The first sentence of the first book, *City of Golden Shadow,* reads, "It started in mud, as many things do."[24]

Start with an emotion. "124 was spiteful."[25]

That's the opening line of *Beloved* by Toni Morrison, which won the Nobel Prize for literature and is truly an incredible book. "124" is a house number, and it begs the question, "How can a house be spiteful?"

Start with humor. *Di and I* by Peter Lefcourt is essentially a rom-com featuring the author and Princess Diana. The first sentence is quite long compared to the others I've used as examples, and I've also included the second sentence since that provides the humorous payoff.

"It occurs to me, as I sit here naked watching the moon paint the faux tile roofs of the houses on Persimmon Avenue and illuminate the off-beige surface of the rented Ford Taurus in which two men with guns sit watching my house, that only a year ago my life was a great deal simpler. For one thing, I wasn't sleeping with the Princess of Wales."[26]

Start with a mystery. "It was a dumb thing to do but it wasn't that dumb."

That's from Robin McKinley's vampire book, *Sunshine*.[27] What was the dumb thing the character did? I'm going to keep reading to find out.

Start with a question. *Anathem* by Neal Stephenson is another extraordinarily long book (clearly, I have a type), and it literally starts with a question: "'Do your neighbors burn one another alive?' was how Fraa Orolo began his conversation with Artisan Flec."[28]

And you can always **start in the middle of things**. "When I had journeyed half of our life's way, I found myself within a shadowed forest, for I had lost the path that does not stray."[29] That, of course, is the opening line of *The Inferno* by Dante Alighieri.

The truth is, the job of your first sentence is to make the reader read the second sentence, and the job of your second sentence is to make the reader read the first paragraph, and the job of your first paragraph is to make the reader read the first page, and the job of the first page is to make the reader read the first chapter. While, yes, your first sentence is important, it does not have to contain the entirety of your story. It only has to extend the invitation to keep reading.

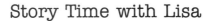

Story Time with Lisa

When I walked into Barnes and Noble that day, I didn't have anything specific in mind, so I made a beeline to my favorite section to browse: fantasy.

Once there, I saw a display of *The Name of the Wind* by Patrick Rothfuss. I wasn't familiar with the author, but the book had an interesting cover and an interesting title. Plus, it was a huge hardback, and as someone who has bought books based solely on the width of the spine, this caught my attention.

I picked up the book, appreciated the heft of it, and flipped it over. The back cover had a list of endorsements from other authors, many of whom I recognized as favorites of mine. Intrigued, I opened the flap and read the jacket.

Jacket flap copy is traditionally written in third-person present tense, with a narrator giving the highlights of the story contained within. This copy was written from the main character's point of view and gave a boastful description of himself and his many accomplishments.

Now I *had* to read the first page, which was a one-page prologue. The first line says simply, "It was night again." I read through the whole page, standing there in the bookstore. Then I got to the last paragraph, which said:

"The Waystone was his, just as the third silence was his. This was appropriate, as it was the greatest silence of the three, wrapping the others inside itself. It was deep and wide as autumn's ending. It was heavy as a great river-smooth stone. It was the patient, cut-flower sound of a man who is waiting to die."[30]

I could not buy the book fast enough. The title was interesting, and so was the jacket copy. The first line was intriguing, but the last line of the prologue sealed the deal.

STARTING STRONG

Your story is more than a single sentence on a single page.

Which is why you shouldn't try to tell your whole story in the first line; you're going to have hundreds and hundreds of pages to tell your story.

That said, you also don't want to start your story in the wrong spot. That is hard advice because how do you know where the right place is to start your story? The easy answer is, "Start in the middle of the action," and while there is a kernel of truth in that, I think it can also trip up an unwary author.

If you start too early, the reader has to slog through a lot of mundane details before we get to the interesting part.

And if you start smack-dab in the middle of the action—in the middle of the car crash, so to speak—we might not care enough about the characters yet to care about the danger they're in.

I like to start the story on the day when everything changes. What is it about today that is different? One way to structure the opening is by "breaking the normal." The story begins with a quick glimpse into the normal day for the character, but then you break that normal by showing us the inciting incident—the event that changes the story.

A quick word of warning: starting with "the normal" doesn't mean you start with your character waking up in bed, getting dressed, going downstairs for breakfast, and then going to school. It means that you'll show us how something in the character's life works normally, and then you'll introduce something that is *not* normal and show us how your character reacts to that.

For example, if you are writing a dystopian story where your main character lives in a school that is highly regimented and where physical contact is forbidden, you could start your story with the character marching in a single-file line to lunch (a normal event) only to see two people secretly holding hands beneath the table (breaking the normal).

You may have found or heard a lot of rules about where and how to start a story. I have listed a few of them myself.

One rule might say that you should never start with the description of the weather. That might be good advice, but what if it's the first time it's rained in 400 years? Another rule I've heard is that you should always start with dialogue. I've also heard that you should never start with an overly detailed description. If dialogue is your strength, feel free to start your book with it. Likewise, if you have a talent for vivid descriptions, use all the adjectives you please to set the opening stage.

I would encourage you to start where you feel most comfortable, where you can showcase your hero, where you can celebrate the elements of storytelling that you are best at, and where you can lead us naturally into the action of the story.

If you're still feeling the pressure of crafting the perfect first sentence, my advice is to not write it first. Write something else, take a break, start with chapter two, give yourself permission to move past the first page. You can always come back and write it later; no one will ever know.

Story Time with Lisa

I knew exactly how I wanted to start *The Hourglass Door*. Because it was a time-travel story to the future, I wanted a prologue from Dante's point of view, set 500 years prior to the main action. But I didn't know what that scene looked like; I didn't know anything except that it would have Dante in it. And I didn't write it for a long, long time. I was nearly halfway through my draft, and my first page was still entirely blank.

I was waiting for the train to take me home after work one day when the opening line hit me: "It is the counting that saves him."[31] I suddenly felt the scene unfolding inside me, the words bubbling up; it was literally a physical sensation. The train pulled up, and I got on. I didn't have my laptop with me, but I did have a notebook and pen, so I wrote the opening scene of my book by hand. The words just flowed. I scratched a few lines out, I wrote a few other sentences in, and by the time the train reached my stop twenty minutes later, I had written the whole prologue to the book.

I went home and typed it up, and I knew it was good.

I called my mom and read it to her, and what ended up being printed in the book was 95 percent exactly the same as what I'd written that day on the train.

But I couldn't have done it if I hadn't allowed myself to become immersed in the world and the story before I attempted to write the prologue. I didn't know what it looked like—until I *did*.

MAKE TIME FOR A PIZZA PARTY

Before you set sail across that daunting and vast blank first page, remember to take a deep breath and have fun. Writing should be fun. Storytelling should be fun. The creative process should be fun. Even revisions can be fun.

Writing a first draft is like making a pizza when you've never made pizza before. But you've had pizza a zillion times, so you know how it should taste.

You make the dough, put the different toppings on, run it through the oven. Then you let your friend try it, and they say, "This dough is too chewy, the sauce needs more oregano, these toppings taste like pickles, and there's not enough cheese—and why is there a LEGO brick in the crust?"

Since this is your first attempt at making pizza, you know it needs work. But it still burns to hear it.

So, you can either quit, never trying to make pizza again, or you can go back and rework it—dough, toppings, more heat—and see how it tastes after that.

After all, what's better than pizza?

Nothing. Nothing is better than pizza.

Chapter 2
The Mathematics of Great Writing

Regardless of the genre you are writing in, this formula is a way to visualize the various parts of a story and how they relate to each other:

PLOT {character [(goal + stakes) + (motivation > adversity)] + conflict [(relationship x stress)] x (try – fail cycles)} + THEME = STORY

Don't panic! It looks complicated, but simply put, you need a character who has a high-stakes goal and motivation greater than whatever adversity they might encounter. Add conflict, which is created when relationships are placed under multiple stressors. Having the characters work to resolve that conflict through multiple try/fail cycles creates plot. Add theme to this plot and you end up with a story.

Let's talk about each element in the equation in turn, starting with characters and how to develop them.

BUILDING BETTER CHARACTERS

The Mr. Potato Head Way

In my basement is a giant bucket filled with Mr. Potato Head parts that I've somehow accumulated over the years.

I love how easy it is to create endless characters simply by changing out Mr. Potato Head's eyes, ears, hat, mustache, or shoes.

There's something to be said for identifying a character by their clothes—by their external appearance. If you were building Mr. Potato Head to be the hero of the story, he might sport a broad grin and a red cape. A Mr. Potato Head who is more of a geek might wear a pair of glasses, have buck teeth, and don tennis shoes. While a "wicked stepmother" Mrs. Potato Head might choose purple earrings and the eyes with long lashes.

What we see on the outside of a character can help us understand who they are. But it's what's on the inside that helps us understand who they *could* be—and who they want to be.

When you're building a character for the first time, consider all the different parts of the Mr. Potato Head toy and how they might help you dig deeper to create characters who are fully three-dimensional.

Eyes

I always laugh at the line from *Toy Story 2* when Mrs. Potato Head tells Mr. Potato Head, "I'm packing you an extra pair of shoes, and your angry eyes, just in case!"[1]

We often make a point of noting the eye color of our characters, but I would encourage you to instead ask yourself, "What does my character see?"

When they look outside their home, do they see a sprawling urban environment or the vast fields of the countryside? Is the society they belong to large or small? Are the opportunities presented to them vast or limited?

Then take a look inside. What does your character believe about themselves? Do they believe in themself? How confident are they? How much introspection do they need? Do they act first and think later?

How do they see the world around them? Is their perspective one of rose-colored glasses? Or do they see the world with paranoia?

If you can identify what they see in the beginning, you'll know what details they should notice later when their viewpoint or setting changes.

For example, I set *After Hello* in New York, but I wanted my main female protagonist, Sara, to be from Arizona because it does not have the same bustling, big-city skyscraper energy that New York does. That way, when she arrived in the city, she would notice the buildings, the noise, and the lack of a horizon. It allowed me to do some natural world-building because everything she was seeing was new to her.

Ears

Mr. Potato Head usually comes with standard pink ears—sometimes with earrings. But again, ask the question, "What does my character hear?"

A character who has grown up hearing compliments will behave differently from a character who has grown up hearing only criticism. How does what your character hears influence their view of the world, their view of others, and their view of themselves?

And how does your character internalize what they hear? Do they immediately accept the information as truth, or do they suspect it is a lie?

Story Time with Lisa

Many years ago, I had a complicated relationship with a co-worker. We weren't mean to each other, but we also weren't overly friendly. I tried to maintain a professional relationship, but I could never quite figure out why they behaved toward me the way they did.

One day, after our publishing team's weekly meeting, this person said, "Could I take a minute to share something?"

They relayed an experience they'd had with one of their authors, who, after finishing an edit, had told them that working with them had been the best experience this author had ever had.

We all immediately recognized the compliment as being high praise and being the truth.

But what my coworker said was, "Of course, it wasn't true. Besides, adulation is poison."

I literally dropped the pen I was holding because I immediately thought, "That's why they don't ever say anything nice to me. Because they don't see compliments as helpful but hurtful."

It changed how I viewed them and our relationship because I realized that what they heard and what they believed about the world didn't have anything to do with me at all.

Mouth

Mr. Potato Head has a variety of mouth options, from bucktooth smiles to a tongue sticking straight out. But I want you to think about what your character says.

When do they speak and when do they choose to be silent? Are they thoughtful about their words? Or do they blurt out their emotions without consideration or regard? Is their silence a sign of fear? Or is it a weapon they wield as revenge or as punishment?

How do they speak? Is it formal, or do they use slang or inside jokes or language that only a few people would understand?

Dialogue can reveal a character's educational levels, their beliefs, their prejudices, and their personality.

Writing compelling dialogue can be daunting. You want your characters to sound like real people, but have you ever tried to transcribe an actual conversation between two people? Those conversations can be filled with fragment sentences, wandering stories that may or may not have a point, or even inside jokes or references that are nearly indecipherable without the proper context. Conversation is rarely straightforward, though there may be a time and place for that in your story. Feel free to utilize subtext, evasive language, questions with delayed answers, or even banter to give your dialogue life and personality.

My advice for writing dialogue is to make it matter. Whatever your character says should either help further the plot or reveal something about a character. As you get to know your characters better, you'll have a deeper understanding of what their voice sounds like.

We all use different language depending on who we're talking to. Imagine a sixteen-year-old girl, and her mom asks, "How was your day at school?" The girl's answer might be a noncommittal, "Fine." But that same girl, asked that same question by her best friend, might respond by opening a floodgate of gossip and excitement and secret fears and triumphs. And when that same question is asked by the girl's mortal enemy, she might reply with a question of her own: "Why do you care?"

I also like to do a reading pass of a manuscript in which I read only the dialogue out loud. That helps me hear the differences in the various characters' voices as well as gives me a sense of the pacing. If I find that there are long stretches of silence between lines of dialogue, that could indicate a slower-paced section, which might be fine if the scene is introspective. But if I am looking for a fast-paced scene, I'll want to tighten the narration so the dialogue flows faster.

Arms

Mr. Potato Head has two little, bendy, white arms that stick into the sides of his rotund Potato Head body. When you think about your character's arms, I want you to think about what your character is reaching for. What are the things that would be "nice to have" versus the things they "have to have"?

Story Time with Lisa

When my first book was coming out, I had the opportunity to go to BookExpo America, a national trade show for publishers to showcase their new titles. Not only would it be my first time going to BEA, but it would also be my first time going to New York.

Which meant, before I got there, I needed to go shopping.

Which I hate.

I am a very tall person, and I rarely find clothes in the store that fit me. I also see clothes as more functional than fashionable, so I never quite know what looks good on me. But I took a deep breath and went to an upscale store to buy a nice pair of pants. After much searching and many hours, I finally found a pair that fit. Then I looked at the price tag; it was three digits.

I thought to myself, *You want* how much *for a pair of pants?*

And a little voice in the back of my head immediately spoke up and said, "Yes, and that's almost the exact same amount you paid for concert tickets to see Rush in Las Vegas for the seventeenth time."

That was when I realized I would rather spend my money on an experience than on a possession. Pants are pants; they shouldn't cost that much. But the chance to see my favorite band play live in Vegas? Now, *that* I would pay for willingly, without hesitation.

For me, tailored pants were something that would be "nice to have," but the concert was something I "had to have."

The experience got me thinking, and when I got home, I posted this on Facebook: "Hypothetical situation: You have $500. Would you buy new clothes for a business trip, or would you pay to see your favorite band in concert? Those are your only two choices."

Despite my explicit instructions, everybody offered different answers: "I would give it to charity." "I would pay my bills." "I would buy books."

What we each find important can be vastly different. For some people, it's possessions; for others, it's experiences. If your character had $500, what would they buy?

When identifying and establishing dreams, the more specific you can be, the better. I didn't just want to see my favorite band in concert; I wanted to see Rush in Las Vegas for the seventeenth time. I wasn't just buying pants for a trip to New York City; I was attending a national book trade show to promote the release of my first book, *The Hourglass Door*. The more specific you can be about what your character is reaching for, what they are dreaming of, the more well-rounded they will be.

Legs

Mr. Potato Head doesn't have legs, except in the movies. But think about your character's legs and ask, "Where are you going?"

Will your character's path lead them from weakness to strength (Bruce Wayne in *Batman Begins*) or from strength to a different kind of strength (Bruce Wayne in *The Dark Knight*)?

What action are they willing to take to get what they want? Will they lie, cheat, or steal? Will they become stronger? Brave enough to forgive? Will they become more capable and welcome the growing pains that come with it? Will they ask anybody for help?

Feet

When you look at Mr. Potato Head's shoes, ask, "What does your character stand for?"

What makes your character truly happy? What are the things they want? What are the things they dream of? What will they fight for—even die for?

Your job as the author is simply to prove it by putting your character in situations where they will have to fight for or possibly even die for the things they need, the things they want, the things they wish for, the things they dream of.

"Three Is a Magic Number"

One final piece to the character puzzle is turning a character's flaw into a strength. Readers are rooting for your character to overcome their weaknesses and to find opportunities to showcase their heroic qualities.

One quick technique that I use when I'm starting a new project is to think about my character and write down three wishes, three fears, three flaws, and three heroic qualities.

Sometimes those elements will dovetail. Perhaps what they're wishing for is the opposite of what they fear. They wish for connection because they fear abandonment. Perhaps they wish for a forgiving heart because they are quick to anger. Perhaps they wish for courage because that is a heroic quality they feel they lack.

Once you have identified all twelve characteristics, you can extrapolate from them a "shopping list" of scenes that you will need in your book.

Those three wishes? Deny them.

Those three fears? Manifest them.

Those three strengths? Weaken them.

Those three flaws? Exploit them.

Protagonists and Antagonists

Now that you have thought about your character's eyes, ears, mouth, arms, legs, and feet and have identified their three wishes, fears, flaws, and heroic qualities, it's time to ask some additional questions to shape your character into a protagonist or an antagonist.

While Mr. Potato Head doesn't wear pants, if he did, he would need a BELT: beliefs, emotions, loyalties, and traits.

Beliefs

What is the foundational stone of your character's belief system? Perhaps your character believes in God, but is it a positive or negative relationship? Or perhaps there isn't any relationship at all, and they only believe in their own talent or sense of confidence. Perhaps the foundational stone of their belief is the idea that love triumphs.

How much pain can they withstand before they abandon that belief?

Push your characters to their own personal limits in order to find that moment when they say, "I can't go past this line. I *won't* go past this line." Then you either have to find what motivation will force them to cross it, or you reward them for remaining true to their values.

Emotions

How can we share in a character's feelings if we don't know what they are? The internet has some excellent "emotion wheels" that list layers of emotions beyond "good" or "bad."

Your character might have moved past "sad" and into "lonely." They might wish to not only be loved but also feel valued. Perhaps your character's anger stems from their jealousy. Diving deep into emotional descriptions and definitions can add texture to your character's complexity and can inspire greater empathy in the reader.

What unexpected fear does your main character have?

In season one of *Supernatural*, we meet Dean Winchester, and we quickly learn he doesn't appear to be afraid of anything—not ghosts, not wendigos, not monsters in the lake. But by episode four, when he and his brother, Sam, must board a plane, we see that he is, in fact, terrified of something: flying.

That unexpected fear is both humorous and immediately endearing. It gives us a hint into Dean's inner life, a glimpse behind the armor he wears to protect himself from the world. It also explains why he and Sam drive everywhere in their 1967 Chevy

Impala. The story of *Supernatural* would be very different if the Winchesters could simply hop on a plane and travel from Kansas to Oregon to California to Florida.

Another question to ask might be: What has your character done that they feel guilty about? And can they atone for it? Even if the answer is no, that doesn't mean your character will stop trying to achieve it.

What does your character need to feel after they defeat the villain: relief, sadness, elation? What will bring them closure? At the end of *Avengers: Endgame*, when Tony Stark has used the last of his energy and strength to snap his fingers and destroy Thanos, there is a sense of relief and sadness along with the victory.

Layering emotions and using more descriptive and specific words for emotions can help create memorable and poignant scenes in your story.

Loyalties

Who does your character call for help? Who's first on their speed dial, and what does that relationship look like? What does that relationship say about your character?

Where does your character go to feel safe? This could be a physical place, or it could be a mental or imaginary place.

What kind of reputation does your character hold in the community? Is your character Gaston from *Beauty and the Beast*? Or Clark Kent in Metropolis?

And when it comes to your antagonist, remember that they can't be pure evil. Give us a reason why someone could admire or love them. Who is your villain's best friend? How did they become friends? Why do they stay friends?

What legacy does your character want to leave behind—and what legacy will they *actually* leave behind?

Some of the answers to these questions may not appear anywhere in your story, and that's okay, but answering them can help you as the writer understand your character's perspective and viewpoint better, which will allow you to more authentically write how your character will react and behave in certain situations.

Traits

We've talked about heroic qualities already, so for this one, I like to ask, "Who is my hero's hero?" Then I make a list of the heroic qualities of my main character's idol and think about the ways in which my hero emulates those qualities and the ways in which they fail to live up to them.

Building Better Antagonists

Everything about developing a protagonist—their history, insights, beliefs, emotions, loyalties, traits, and physical characteristics—should also be applied when developing your antagonist because your antagonist should be as well-formed, well-developed, and interesting as your protagonist.

In short: Your bad guys should be really good at their jobs.

Like protagonists, antagonists should be smart, crafty, manipulative, daring, bold, memorable, and terrifying. They should have in-depth backstories and character arcs. They should have plans and goals, and they should demonstrate growth—even if the growth of your antagonist is into a more sinister complexity.

Questioning Your Villain

Could your villain be the hero of their own story? If every great hero is defined by their villain, then take some time to question the relationship between your protagonist and antagonist.

When it comes to Batman and Joker, the Joker's goal isn't just to stop Batman or be an annoyance to him, though he is certainly happy when that happens. The Joker wants to create chaos, which he can do with or without Batman in the picture. What is it about the Joker that allows him to rise to the level of arch-nemesis so that

Batman must utilize all his skills and abilities to defeat him? Is your villain worthy of your hero's time, attention, and talents?

As the Terminator, Arnold Schwarzenegger looks human but is actually a cyborg on a mission to assassinate Sarah Connor. The machine is intimidating, relentless, and unemotional. But for the sequel, *Terminator 2: Judgment Day*, the cyborg has undergone some serious upgrades. The T-1000 is still intimidating, relentless, and unemotional—but now it is made of liquid metal that allows it to shapeshift into various forms, transform its limbs into weapons, and reform after nearly any physical damage. Is your villain increasing in strength, danger, and power?

Consider Clarice Starling and Hannibal Lecter. How does your villain know about your hero's weaknesses, their past, or their secrets?

How would your villain describe and define your hero? Perhaps your villain feels as Belloq does in *Raiders of the Lost Ark* when he says to Indiana Jones, "I am a shadowy reflection of you. It would take only a nudge to make you like me, to push you out of the light."[2]

What Do They Have to Lose?

When it comes to the threat level between your antagonist and your protagonist, try to go past the obvious to uncover the true inner threat that the villain poses to your hero.

What will your protagonist lose (besides possibly their life) if they go up against the antagonist and fail? Will they lose hope, faith, confidence, identity, respect, love? Make sure to continually raise the stakes by making them personal. Make the threat matter.

One of my favorite characters is the Doctor from *Doctor Who*. The Doctor is a Time Lord who periodically regenerates into a new body—either male or female—which is how they live such a long life. Throughout time, however, two groups of antagonists continue to pose the greatest threats to the Doctor: the Cybermen and the Daleks.

Whenever the Doctor regenerates, there's a moment where the Doctor stands up and makes a pronouncement about who they are and why the enemy should be afraid of them. The other main characteristic of the Doctor, aside from their very clear sense of identity regardless of what body they are currently inhabiting, is their longevity. The Doctor will always be the Doctor for hundreds of years, thousands of years; the Doctor is eternal.

Thus, the specific threat of the Cybermen is assimilation—the Doctor will lose their identity and become just like everybody else. And the Daleks' war cry is "Exterminate!" Not just *kill* but *exterminate*—to put an end to something that is endless.

Those specific threats make those antagonists even more dangerous to the Doctor because they both strike right at the heart (or in the case of the Doctor, their double hearts) of what makes that character so powerful.

Clothes Make the Man

We've talked about developing the inner life of a character, but as I mentioned at the beginning of this section, the internal qualities of your character can be connected to the external. In other words, what your character wears can symbolize their personality or reflect who they are on the inside.

Pay attention to what your character is wearing. What does it say about them? What might it symbolize about their personality? When you change up their clothes, consider how that might change up their inner self as well.

Imagine two men: one in a sharp, three-piece suit, and the other in ragged pants and bare feet. Who do we assume is the dominant character in that scene? What might their clothes reveal about their history or their future?

There's a reason we wear "power ties" and "power suits" when we go for a job interview. There's a reason we wear sweats and slippers when we need to feel cozy or comforted. There's a reason we wear jeans to a ballgame and a gown to a fancy dinner. Clothes matter. You can make them matter to your character as well.

CHOOSING GOALS AND MOTIVATION

Jurassic Park III has a clear example of character goals and motivation. Dr. Alan Grant essentially says, "I'm never going back to that island," and the other character replies, "Here's a blank check," and they smash cut to everybody on the plane going to the island to be eaten by dinosaurs.

Everyone has a price—even your characters.

Janice Hardy wrote, "Characters drive the plot, because they want something badly enough to act to achieve (or avoid) it. . . . *What* they choose to do is going to create the plot. *Why* they choose to do it will create the motivations and stakes."[3]

Choosing the "What": Goals

Your characters have to want something in order to get the story moving.

Most likely, you will have one primary story goal, but you will also have lots of smaller goals your character will either reach or abandon throughout the story. Changing goals is part and parcel of the classic try/fail cycle because every time a goal changes, the story moves forward, becoming more layered and complex.

Remember the list you made of your character's three wishes, fears, flaws, and heroic qualities? I'll bet you a dollar that at least one of those twelve items can become the primary story goal while the rest can be folded in as secondary goals.

When identifying and evaluating character goals, make sure to include internal and external goals since both will need to be resolved at the story's climax.

Beauty Reborn, by Elizabeth Lowham, is a lovely example of how a character's internal and external goals can both support each other and change throughout the story. In the beginning of this fairy-tale retelling, Beauty's internal goal is what you might expect from a young girl with a heart full of whimsy: she wants to be loved.

But when Stephan wants more from Beauty than she is willing to give, he doesn't take no for an answer, which means that Beauty's internal goal (to be loved) changes and leads directly to a new external goal (to escape Stephan by running into the woods):

"It's true what the folktale says: I did choose to live with the beast. But not for the reason you think. Not to save my father. Not even to save myself.

"In truth, I was hoping I'd be eaten."[4]

As Beauty learns to live with the Beast, her goals change yet again. Beauty's internal goal becomes "to find strength in healing," and her external goal becomes "to save the Beast."

The two goals find completion at the climax of the story when Beauty realizes she is no longer burdened by the trauma she had suffered and that she is strong enough—and vulnerable enough—to give her heart to the Beast, which, of course, saves him from the curse placed on him.

Beauty has other goals throughout the story as well, including "see my family again" and "mend the relationship with my sister." Each goal is connected to the next, like stepping stones across a river, leading Beauty safely through to the story's conclusion.

Let's Go to Disneyland!

Sometimes it's helpful to break down a plot by looking at the choices and consequences that accompany the pursuit of a goal.

- Step one: Set a goal.
- Step two: Identify the steps required to reach the goal and the obstacles your character might encounter.
- Step three: List the choices your character must make to overcome those obstacles.

- Step four: Push the limit. Do the choices escalate in difficulty? Do they demand a higher and higher cost?
- Step five: Apply consequences. List five possible consequences for each choice, then write one (or all) of them.

For example, let's set a goal to go to Disneyland.

When we make a list of steps required to make the trip, we can immediately come up with a list of obstacles that will make reaching our goal difficult. Our list might include problems such as we can't afford it, we don't have the time, we're not interested in going to Disneyland, we suffer from motion sickness, or we have a deep-seated fear of a human-sized mouse wearing pants and shoes, trying to convince us to buy a five-dollar-and-fifty-cent churro.

From that list, let's pick one obstacle that we'll need to resolve. We can't afford to go to Disneyland, so step one of our goal is *get more money*.

How could we get more money? Let's make another list. We could get a loan from the bank—or rob it. We could ask our parents for money. We could hold a garage sale or sell a kidney on the black market or save up our spare change over a period of time. Some of the choices are clearly better than others; some of them are more legal than others.

Let's pick one of those choices and then apply the consequences.

Our goal is to get to Disneyland.

To accomplish that, we need more money.

To get more money, we are going to rob a bank.

In order to rob a bank, we'll need to have a plan that includes knowledge of the bank's hours, knowledge of the bank personnel, somebody who can open the safe, somebody who can reroute the closed-circuit security cameras, and somebody who can drive the getaway car.

Now, all of a sudden, we have more goals to deal with along with more choices and more consequences of those choices. One consequence of robbing a bank might be being chased by the police, arrested, and tossed into jail.

But since our primary goal is still to get to Disneyland, now we have to figure out how to escape from jail.

(Also: This is how you build a try/fail cycle, which is when a character tries to accomplish a goal, fails, and then must try something else later to reach the same goal. Ideally, you will also weave in some try/succeed cycles as well so that your character can grow.)

Stakes

The stakes matter when the relationships matter. It's one thing to say the world will be destroyed, which is an external stake, but it's another thing to say, "If the world is destroyed, then my mom will also die." That becomes much more personal, much more relevant, and much more powerful. It is also an internal stake. We may intellectually understand why it would be bad for the world to be destroyed, but we feel immediately in our hearts why it would be worse for a loved one to die.

Look at the choices your character needs to make, especially at the end of the story. Are they life or death? Should they be? Could they be?

One way to raise the stakes is by demanding a sacrifice. Ask your character to make a sacrifice at the beginning of the story, then ask them to make the same sacrifice at the end. What has changed in the reaction and response to that request then and now? Why?

Ultimately, stakes are the result of the questions: What is the consequence of failure? Does the outcome, good or bad, carry enough emotional weight to make the journey worth it?

Choosing the "Why": Motivation

Often, I find that when I am not engaged with the character, it's because I don't understand their motivation. I don't know *why* they're doing what they're doing, so I don't care about *what* they're doing.

Mark Nichol wrote, "Only after you decide what your character wants, what your character needs, what your character must have—or he or she will die physically or psychologically—only then should you discover how he or she is going to go about getting it."[5]

What your character wants, needs, and must have could all be the same, or they could all be different. If you, as the author, can clearly articulate each of those facets, you will know how to grant your character what they want or what they need or what they must have—or you will know how to withhold them. In fact, the granting and withholding of those wants and needs can motivate your character into action, and a character in action carries your plot.

With proper motivation, you can make your characters do anything.

For example, what would motivate your protagonist to kill somebody they love? At first glance, the answer may be nothing, but what if the person the character loved was terminal and suffering; could they do it then, as an act of mercy? What if the person they loved had been turned into a zombie? What if there was abuse in the relationship and the death came from self-defense?

Those are all very different motivations, and we, as readers, may agree or disagree with them, but we should at least understand why that character chose what they did.

Creating Strong Choices

A strong choice creates strong motivation. It's often easy to choose between two good options. Would you rather have $1 million or $1 billion? Either choice might be good for your bank account, but it doesn't make for a compelling plot point for your story.

It's also not that difficult to choose between a good thing and a bad thing. Would you rather have $1 million or spend eight hours getting five root canals with no anesthesia? (Perhaps with $1 million, you could afford a new toothbrush once in a while.)

What becomes really compelling is when you have to choose between two bad things or when you have to choose between two good things that are in conflict.

Randy Ingermanson recommended having your character complete the following statement: "Nothing is more important than X, except Y."

(More math? I know. I'm sorry.)

He continues: "Most people can give you two or three things that they think should go in the blank. . . . A strong story comes from putting those in conflict."[6]

Some answers for those variables might include respect, family, God, money, health, vengeance, or love.

What values or ideals does your character hold that they judge to be equally important? What will they do when they are forced to choose between them?

In *Supernatural*, Dean Winchester would say, "Nothing is more important than the family business of hunting monsters—except for protecting my brother, Sam." So what will Dean do when Sam turns into a monster?

In the first episode of *Breaking Bad*, Walter White makes a recording where he says, "My name is Walter Hartwell White. . . . This is not an admission of guilt. I am speaking to my family now. . . . I just want you to know that no matter how it may look, I only had [all three of] you in my heart."[7]

Throughout the course of the show, as we follow his transformation from high school chemistry teacher with lung cancer to kingpin drug lord, we hear him repeat this belief: "Everything I'm doing is for my family."

Until in the last episode, when he has nothing left to lose, he finally admits the truth, which is, "I did it for me. I liked it. I was good at it. And I was really . . . . I was alive."[8]

Thus Walter White would say, "Nothing is more important than providing for my family—except for getting the respect I deserve."

Imagine a fulcrum with the center point being the inciting incident. On the left-hand side is where you start gathering energy, so to speak. Ask your character, "What do you value?" Then back up a step and say, "What happened in your past to establish those beliefs and values? What experiences did you have that created the belief that you currently hold about what is important to you?"

Then, on the right-hand side of that fulcrum is where you can expend that energy into driving your character forward. Ask your character, "What do you want? And how will you know when you're successful? What does victory look like when you uphold your values or when you reach your goal?"

What happened to establish beliefs and values?	What do I value?	**STORY BEGINS**	What do I want?	How will I know when I am successful?
↑	↑	↑	↑	↑

Gather Energy	Expend Energy

First Aid for Character Ennui

What if your characters still don't seem to have the requisite motivation to get up off the page and do something interesting? They're standing around looking at each other, saying, "What do you want to do now?" And the other character says, "I don't know. What do you want to do?"

Drawing up the principles of basic first aid,[9] here are three Cs to cure your character of ennui.

The first thing you should do when you're in a dangerous situation is **check your surroundings**. You can do the same thing with your character: evaluate the situation they're in and identify the danger in the setting. If you're applying true first aid, you would mitigate that danger, but since you are applying motivation, you instead exploit that danger.

The second step is to **call for help**. In a real situation, you would call for a doctor, the police, or first responders. Is there someone your character could call to help solve the problem? If yes, consider preventing that person from arriving. If no, then feel free to pile on the problems until your character is forced into action.

The third step in basic first aid is to **care for the person**. Have them sit, give them a glass of water, and wrap them in a blanket to help with the shock. In your story, after the danger's past and the problem has been solved, let your character know that they're going to be all right. Give them a moment of success, allow them to catch their breath . . . and then introduce another danger or another problem.

Lather. Rinse. Repeat.

INCREASING CONFLICT BY TRIANGULATING CHARACTER RELATIONSHIPS

Jim Butcher once taught a four-hour workshop at the Superstars Writing Seminar in Colorado, and he started his presentation with a rather throwaway comment: "Conflict is what happens between characters."

I sat back in my seat, stunned at the simplicity and the truth of that statement. It wasn't a brand-new idea to me, but I had never heard it articulated quite that way before.

He went on to talk about the difference between conflict and adversity, which I had always used interchangeably, but the more I thought about it and the more I studied it, the more I believed that Jim was right. There is a difference, and that difference comes down to relationships.

Since conflict requires more than one character, it means someone is actively working against your character in a scene. But that person doesn't always have to be the antagonist; it can be a friend or a supporting character.

For example, in *Fellowship of the Ring*, the Fellowship must make a choice. Do they go through the Mines of Moria (which is extremely dangerous but a shorter route), or do they go around the mountain (which is less dangerous but will take more time)? At this moment of choice, conflict arises because different people in the Fellowship have different ideas of which way to go, and each character is advocating for their own personal decision. Some of them want to go through the mines; some of them want to go around the mountain, despite the heavy snowstorm.

That is perhaps a low-stakes conflict, but it is conflict nonetheless.

Adversity

As Gandalf and the Fellowship are standing on the mountain, trying to decide which way to go, their choice is taken away from them when an avalanche breaks off and blocks the path. Now they must go through the Mines of Moria. The avalanche got in the way and changed the direction of the story by forcing the characters onto a new path. That is not necessarily conflict; that's adversity.

Other examples of adversity could include other natural disasters, like a forest fire or bad weather. It could be the distance your characters have to travel. Or perhaps time is short, and your character has only an hour to accomplish a task. Perhaps there's a physical constraint hampering a character's movement, like a broken leg or a broken arm. Maybe your protagonist is too young or too old for the job they must do.

Adversity comes in the obstacles your character must overcome. It is a stumbling block, a boulder in the road.

But adversity alone does not naturally bring about conflict, because adversity alone doesn't carry much weight. It's hard to feel emotionally invested in an avalanche, but we do feel emotionally invested in the characters who must deal with the avalanche and the consequences of it. In the same way, we feel the tension of conflict increase when the antagonist introduces adversity as a way to put pressure or strain on the relationship with the protagonist.

Story Time with Lisa

I've been a fan of Christopher Nolan's movies since *Memento*, and I was particularly eager to see his movie *Dunkirk*, which is based on a true story of World War II.

I watched with rapt attention as the British Army retreated from the Germans through occupied France. The soldiers got all the way to the shore, but they had nowhere to go. They were so close, they could practically see England across the water. But the Germans were coming up behind them, and every time the British tried to get on a ship or go down to the beach or attempt a crossing, the German Air Force came in close and shot at them. The British were trapped.

The other side of the story focused on the British citizens—regular people with regular boats—who sailed across the Channel, picked up the soldiers, and brought them home.

It was an amazing story, but I found myself not emotionally invested because it felt like one long series of adverse situations. Yes, stories need obstacles, and plenty of them, but the try/fail cycles were more like fail/fail cycles, and since I didn't know who any of the characters were, I sort of didn't care if they lived or died.

Now, it may be that Christopher Nolan's intent was not to single out one individual to be the protagonist because he wanted to tell the whole story of all the British troops as a group, but though the movie was highly successful, I personally left the theater disappointed.

I contrast that story with the miniseries *Band of Brothers*, which I watch every year on either Veterans Day or Memorial Day weekend when the History Channel shows all ten episodes in a row. That story allows me to experience World War II through the eyes of Easy Company from the 101st Airborne, from D-Day all the way to Hitler's Eagle's Nest. Not only am I introduced to each of these men individually, but I am also deeply invested in their relationships with each other. As those relationships are put under the stress of war, as those men face adversity and hardship, the story naturally carries a high level of tension. It's why I keep coming back to the story.

Adversity is important, but it's hard for a character to be victorious against random bad luck, so be strategic about where and when you employ those obstacles. If your character constantly bumps up against obstacles but never overcomes them, it's hard for us to root for that character to succeed.

Your character will be in pain at some point in the story. That's to be expected, even encouraged. But that pain should have a purpose. Sisyphus rolled a boulder uphill every day only to have it roll back down every night for eternity. There was no point to that struggle; there was no purpose, and so there was no payoff.

You want your hero to eventually be able to roll the rock up the hill and over the edge onto their enemies.

Conflict + Adversity + Changing Relationships

Conflict without adversity can result in low stakes. Adversity without conflict can result in low emotional engagement. But adversity paired with conflict can increase tension, heighten suspense, deepen relationships, and advance the story.

Remember our goal of going to Disneyland? Well, imagine that you have successfully escaped from jail after having robbed a bank to get enough money to finance the trip, and now you are on the road, headed for the Happiest Place on Earth. Riding shotgun with you is your mom (because I guess the family that robs banks together goes to Disneyland together), when suddenly, you get a flat tire! What do you do now?

Now change out the person in the car with you. Same trip. Same flat tire. But now it's you and your boss. Or you and your child. Or you and the hitchhiker you picked up because you were feeling nice. What if Batman and Joker were on a road trip to Disneyland, and they got a flat tire?

The goal is the same. Even the obstacle is the same. But the scene will play out very differently depending on the relationship between the characters.

As you change the relationship, you can change the conflict, but there are pros and cons that come with that change, so you'll want to be smart about how you go about it. If you are changing a relationship from friend to enemy, then you are definitely increasing your conflict opportunities. If you are changing the relationship from enemy to friend, that could be a plot twist—the character you thought was working against you this entire time actually brought the cavalry to save the day at the end of the story. Surprise!

Friends to lovers is one of the standard happily-ever-after tropes of romance novels, but changing from lovers to spouses can lessen the romantic tension because the question "Will they, won't they?" has been answered. Yes, they got married.

Once you define the relationship, whether that is a parent-child relationship, siblings, friends, lovers, enemies, teacher-student, spouses, ex-spouses, boyfriend-girlfriend, strangers, or boss-employee, you can start changing it either in positive ways—bringing the characters closer—or in negative ways—pulling them apart. Relationships under pressure create conflict.

Think of Sam and Frodo and Gollum. Sam and Frodo are friends, but the relationship between Sam and Gollum is one of distrust and suspicion and anger, perhaps even downright hatred. Gollum's relationship with Frodo is built on deceit and manipulation. Likewise, the relationship between Frodo and Smeagol is one of pity. The relationship between Smeagol and Gollum is one of control.

That same trio is a great example of one of the best tools I keep in my writing kit: a triangle.

Triangulating Character Relationships

I opened this chapter with a complicated equation about writing, and now I'm presenting a geometry lesson? I know, this is a book about writing, not math, but trust me.

Why triangles?

Because architecturally, they are often used in bridges to provide strength and stability, which can help you build a strong "plot bridge" to get your characters from point A to point B.

Triangles are also designed to withstand pressure. In writing, pressure is how you raise the stakes, enforce action, increase tension, and generate character growth.

Triangles can also help determine location. If you know two points along a baseline—and their angle measurements—you can calculate where the third point will be. (The process is literally called triangulation.) Thus, using triangles in our writing can help us identify where we are and where we need to go.

Most importantly, triangles present a choice. You've probably heard the phrase "Fast, cheap, or accurate. Pick two." Much of what we have talked about regarding character goals and motivation boils down to making choices. How strongly will your character defend what they believe in? How much pressure can they withstand? Where do you want your character to go, and why?

In a Galaxy Far, Far Away

When I was first learning how stories are put together, my mom used *Star Wars* to help me understand this concept of relationships and choices. She drew a triangle with Luke Skywalker, the protagonist, at one point. She labeled the left corner "Darth Vader" and the right corner "Obi-Wan Kenobi." The triangle structure—and the story that grows from it—clearly puts Luke on a path that will require him to choose between becoming a Jedi Knight or going to the dark side of the Force.

Star Wars

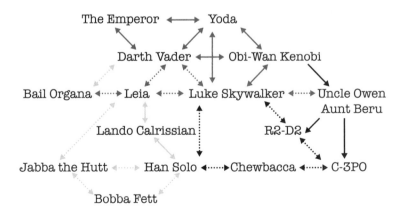

We can build out the story's relationship map to include the other main (and sometimes minor) characters who support the main triangle of Luke, Obi-Wan, and Darth Vader.

For example, the dark-gray solid lines connect the characters centered around the Force (either Jedi or Sith): The Emperor, Yoda, Darth Vader, Obi-Wan Kenobi, and Luke Skywalker. Luke's relationship with each of those characters continues to put pressure (positive and negative) on his decision of what kind of Force-user he will be.

The dark-gray dotted lines connect family relationships: Luke Skywalker, Darth Vader (his father), Leia (his sister), Bail Organa (Leia's adoptive father), and Owen and Beru (Luke's uncle and aunt).

The light-gray solid lines hint at the romance subplot: Leia, Han Solo, and Lando Calrissian. (Let's just ignore the kiss Luke and Leia shared before they knew they were family, shall we?)

The light-gray dotted lines build out subplot conflicts: Jabba the Hutt has hired the bounty hunter Bobba Fett to track down Han Solo for an unpaid debt. Later, in *Return of the Jedi*, Jabba captures Leia, which adds pressure to the relationship she has established with Han Solo. There is also a subplot triangle that connects Darth Vader, Bail Organa, and Leia, since it is the Imperial Death Star that destroys Alderaan.

The dark-black dotted lines denote friendship connections: Luke Skywalker, Han Solo, Chewbacca, and the droids, C-3PO and R2-D2.

You'll notice that there are solid-black lines connecting Uncle Owen and Aunt Beru to the droids, but the arrows only point one way. That's because that relationship is one way. The main function of Owen and Beru's characters is to facilitate getting the droids to Luke—and then dying so Luke can begin his quest as the Chosen One.

I also want to point out that three characters can be connected in a line instead of a triangle. For example, the line that connects

Luke to R2-D2 also connects him to C-3PO. That's important because Luke has individual relationships with both droids. So when you are looking for connections, remember that the three points of a character triangle might not look like a traditional triangle.

It's also important to make sure your main characters have the most arrows pointing to and away from them, meaning that they have the most relationships in the story. On this map, Luke has seven arrows directly connecting him to other characters, whereas Jabba the Hutt has only three.

Once we have identified and defined the relationship triangles, we can begin to change them in order to increase the tension.

In the beginning, Luke's relationship with Obi-Wan is superficial. "Old Ben" is the hermit who lives out in the desert and is not to be taken seriously. But when Luke realizes that Obi-Wan is actually a Jedi Knight, the relationship changes to mentor and student and then to master and apprentice.

We learn from Obi-Wan that Darth Vader killed Luke's father, Obi-Wan's friend, so the relationship between the Sith Lord and the Jedi is rooted in antagonism. Yet later, when we understand more deeply that Obi-Wan and Anakin Skywalker were once best friends and brothers-in-arms, it changes how we see the characters, and we mourn the loss of that relationship. We also see how that broken relationship created tension and conflict, which was part of what drove Anakin to become Darth Vader in the first place.

The relationship between Luke Skywalker and Darth Vader is also antagonistic until the revelation that Darth Vader is actually Luke's father. Plot twist! (We'll talk more about those later.)

Using this method of triangulation, it is easy to make a map of your characters—starting with the protagonist, the antagonist, and the alternate—and define and label the relationships. Next, connect the characters through their emotional needs and extrapolate what their goals might be. Then identify plot points in which you can add adversity in order to change a relationship and create conflict.

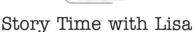

Story Time with Lisa

When I started working on *The Hourglass Door*, I began by creating a relationship map.

Just as my mom taught me, I started with a triangle. Abby was my main character, so she went in the middle. I knew she'd have parents—a mom and a dad—which created a triangle. Abby had a sister, Hannah. Hannah had a couple of friends, Cori and McKenna, which created another triangle. I also knew that Hannah and her friends wouldn't play a large part of the story, but they went on the map anyway.

I added Abby's boyfriend, Jason, and her best friend, Natalie. From that triangle, I added another of Abby's best friends, Valerie.

I added Abby's love interest, Dante, and Dante's brother, Leo. I knew that Zo would be the antagonist, and he would have some henchmen, Tony and V.

As I put all the characters on the map and drew lines connecting them, it helped me see which relationships had weak points built into them and which relationships would stay strong. It also helped me visualize the kinds of scenes I would need in the book. I couldn't just say Abby and Dante were in love. I had to show them building a relationship. That's the point of the romance.

At the same time, I knew I needed scenes in which Abby and Jason's relationship would weaken and break because I needed Abby to realize that she wasn't in love with Jason; she was actually in love with Dante. I couldn't have her dump her existing boyfriend for someone else without good reason; nobody would believe it, and it could make her into an unlikable character. I had to show it. I planned scenes in which Abby and Jason talked about their relationship and in which Abby and Dante talked about their relationship. I picked out story points in which Abby and Dante could go on a date as well as the point in which Abby and Jason break up.

Between my detailed outline and this character relationship map, I cruised through writing a significant portion of the novel. But partway through the book, I started to flounder. I felt like I was missing something, so I went back to my outline. Unsurprisingly, the plot had changed over the course of my writing, so that wasn't much help.

Then I took another look at my character map and asked myself, "Are there any triangles that I can close to create a new relationship to explore?"

The Hourglass Door

Mom
Dad   Cori

Leo ⟷ Abby ⟷ Hannah

Dante ⟷ Jason   McKenna

Zo ⟷ Valerie ⟷ Natalie

Tony ⟷ V

I realized I had created a couple of neighboring triangles:

- Valerie and Dante were friends because they were both connected to Abby.
- Valerie and Zo were connected because Valerie was a fan of Zo's music.
- Zo and Dante were at odds because Dante was trying to protect Abby from Zo.
- Zo and V were in the same band together, but of the two, Zo was clearly the leader.

I quickly saw that I didn't have a relationship between Valerie and V. What would happen if I connected those two characters and created a triangle consisting of Valerie, Zo, and V?

The answer to that question not only changed the course of Valerie's character arc in book one but throughout the entire trilogy.

I realized that Valerie would have been attracted to V, but Zo would have used the power in his relationship with V to supplant him, claim Valerie for himself, and say, "If I can't get to Abby through Dante, I'll get to her through Valerie." That created a high level of tension between these characters as well as an unusual, dysfunctional relationship between Valerie and Zo that was fun to write and fascinating to explore.

If you are stuck in your book or your characters feel adrift, try mapping out relationship triangles. Identify who is on the edge of the map and see if you can draw them into more relationships. It could provide you with interesting subplots, or perhaps even main plots, that could expand your story.

Story Time with Lisa

You can also use this method to identify potential problems with a plot.

I had been assigned to edit an epic fantasy novel for work, and it had a large cast of characters with multiple points of view and multiple plot lines.

I hadn't read the book yet, but my boss had, so he was telling me about the story, some of his favorite scenes, and the characters. I was having trouble trying to keep them all straight, so I got a piece of paper and asked, "Who's the main character? Who's the antagonist? Who are the important people in this person's life?"

I started to map out the characters and their connections, and I kept asking, "Who else is in the book?" I finally had a map of about twenty different people and how they were connected and what their goals were. It took about fifteen minutes, and when I was done, I drew a line straight through the middle of the paper and said, "No one above this line has any relationship to any one below this line, which means no characters from plot line number one cross over and matter in plot line number two. There are two different stories in this book that never intertwine, and that's a problem."

"This is why we pay you the big bucks," my boss said.

I had discovered the problem simply by analyzing the character relationships and making sure everybody had a place on the map—and in the story.

UTILIZING THEME, TENSION, AND TWISTS

One of the other reasons I like to triangulate my character relationships is because when I combine it with "the rule of three," it helps me find places in the story to thread in a theme, tighten the tension, and plan for a plot twist.

The Rule of Three

The rule of three is one that we often follow without thought. It has been present since the earliest stories, and we frequently see it in classic fairy tales. The rule often follows "good, better, best" ("The Three Little Pigs") or "fail, fail, succeed" ("Rumpelstiltskin"). Essentially, the first time something happens, it's interesting. The second time it happens, it establishes a pattern. The third time it happens can either confirm a problem, present a solution, or establish a theme.

This rule also applies when you are looking to strengthen or weaken character relationships. For example, in a romance, the three scenes you focus on could be "flirt, confide, kiss." For a drama, the relationship could be "crack, fracture, break." Or you might have a character approach a puzzle through "learn, practice, solve." As you layer those three key scenes throughout your story, your characters will progress through the plot in natural and interesting ways.

The magic of this rule is in its repetition, which means it's a helpful tool you can use in a number of writing situations.

Theme

If reading the word *theme* gives you PTSD flashbacks to high school English essays, fear not! Weaving a theme into your story doesn't have to be complicated or stressful. Simply choose an element of your story to be symbolic—it could be an object, a place, a color, a sound, a word, or a person—and then find three places in the story where you can highlight it.

The director M. Night Shyamalan is famously deliberate about the use of colors in his movies, ascribing specific emotions or plot points to each one. Where and when he uses those colors matters.

The Seventh Seal by Ingmar Bergman centers the relationship between the knight and Death around the game of chess, the imagery of which is used multiple times throughout the movie. Likewise, the "milk and strawberries" are used to symbolize hope despite adversity.

In *Supernatural*, the 1967 Chevy Impala represents not only the patriarch, John Winchester, but also his two sons, Sam and Dean. The car doubles as their home when they don't have any money to stay in a motel. It also represents the family business of hunting monsters because the tools they use—from bullets to knives to holy water to grenade launchers—are stored in the trunk.

Because we know those details about the Impala, the scene where Dean takes out his grief after his father's death by repeatedly smashing the trunk with a crowbar carries so much more weight. He could have smashed the windshield, but he smashed the trunk. And that matters. Dean isn't trying to destroy the car. He is trying to work through his anger by lashing out at his father, his home, and his job.

The symbols you choose to utilize can work hand in hand with your theme, so be creative and choose the items that matter most to your characters.

What message do you want to communicate to your audience? Perhaps it is "Imagination can take you places" or "Find your magic." Strive to articulate the ideas and symbols that can resonate with a reader and bring them back to your stories time and again.

Tension

Building tension is all about managing information, both the information the character knows and the information the reader knows. I remember talking to my dad about Watergate and him repeating the famous question at the heart of that scandal: "What did he know, and when did he know it?"

It's a question you should constantly be asking about your characters. Your character is going to learn a lot over the course of the story, and *what* they learn is as important as *when* they learn it. If your story's progress is stuck in the "murky middle," consider having a character tell a lie or reveal a truth. Perhaps give your readers a peek behind the curtain and allow them to know a truth the character does not. Both techniques can help increase tension.

One word of caution, however: if your audience knows more than the character does for too long, you run the risk of your reader thinking your character is stupid, and then we'll lose any sympathy we might have had for them because we think they should be smarter than they are.

Another way to build tension is by employing the simple principle of "what you can't see *can* hurt you." In the movie *Jaws*, we don't see the shark for much of the movie, but when we see those three yellow barrels pop up and head directly for the boat, our hearts beat a touch faster.

Story Time with Lisa

My Aunt Geraldine was a fearless explorer and adventurer in her youth. She climbed Mount Kilimanjaro, drove around South America in a four-wheel-drive truck, went on a walking safari in Africa, and traveled through India. As a child, I loved to listen to her tell her stories, and one of my favorites was "The Wolves of the Yukon."

One night, Geraldine was awakened by the sound of something snuffling around her camp. The creature came closer, and she could see a giant shadow through the thin material of her tent. Then another shadow. And a third. She realized the wild wolves had been drawn by the sound of her ticking alarm clock and had come to investigate.

She lay still and quiet and very much awake in her sleeping bag, listening to the wolves howl. She could both smell and feel the hot breath of the wolf who crouched mere inches away from her all night. When morning came, the wolves finally drifted away, leaving behind only their huge footprints circling her tent.

It's possible to enhance tension by not showing us the monster at all but by simply showing us the shadows in the moment and the footprints left behind.

Ticking clocks are an easy way to build tension. Simply set a deadline by which a goal must be accomplished, and then condense the timeline or add more obstacles to make it more difficult for your character to reach the goal.

A great way to introduce tension is by having a character make an important decision based on misinformation. In *The Dark Knight*, the Joker has captured both Harvey Dent and Rachel Dawes, forcing Batman to make a choice. The clock is ticking, and Batman can save only one. He picks Rachel, and the Joker gives him an address. But when Batman arrives, he finds Harvey instead. The Joker lied about which hostage was at which location because he knew what Batman would choose.

Effective foreshadowing can elevate tension. In *The Shining*, there's a shot of Jack Nicholson's character studying a miniature replica of the hedge maze that surrounds the hotel. At the beginning of the movie, we think it's just a cool maze. But by the end of the story, when Jack Torrance is chasing his son, Danny, through that very same hedge maze in the snow, we realize that what had once been innocent and interesting has now become a deadly threat. The maze is also a great image to evoke the twists and turns of madness that Jack experiences during the story.

Twists

When planning a plot twist, you want to aim for a reader to react with a delighted whisper of, "I knew it," and not an eye roll with, "Oh, come on."

Bad plot twists can happen when the story suffers from insufficient foreshadowing, weak character motivations, clumsy coincidences, and predictable deus ex machina.

How can you effectively pull off a plot twist? One way is by following these five steps.

- ◆ Step one: Set expectations.
- ◆ Step two: Introduce the new idea obliquely.
- ◆ Step three: Falsely confirm the original expectation.

- Step four: Reveal the twist.
- Step five: Provide a believable explanation for the twist.

In *Star Wars: A New Hope*, we set the expectation that Darth Vader is a very bad man. He is strong in the Force. He is ruthless, and he is not a man to be trifled with nor crossed. He will choke a soldier to get the information he needs, and no one will stop him.

We introduce the new idea that Luke Skywalker's father was a Jedi and strong in the Force when Obi-Wan tells Luke, "This is your father's lightsaber."

Then Obi-Wan falsely confirms the original expectation, which is that Darth Vader and Luke Skywalker's father are two separate people. Luke asks, "How did my father die?" and Obi-Wan says, "A young Jedi named Darth Vader. . . . He betrayed and murdered your father."[10]

But then the twist is revealed in *The Empire Strikes Back* when Darth Vader says to Luke, "No, I am your father."[11] (Gasp!)

The last step is to provide a believable explanation. Without backstory or context, we won't believe the twist, and we'll feel like we've been tricked. Thus, after the twist, Luke says in *Return of the Jedi*, "I am a Jedi, like my father before me,"[12] symbolizing that for Luke, he acknowledges that his father was both a Jedi *and* Darth Vader, and he has accepted that as the truth—and so do we.

"STORY" WITH A CAPITAL *S*

I sometimes talk about "Story" with a capital *S* because some stories transcend paper and pen and take root deep in our hearts. Some Stories help us make sense of our life or manage our pain or celebrate our successes.

I hope you found some tools in this chapter to help you, because *your* story is important. Perhaps *your* story can even change—or save—a life.

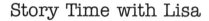

Story Time with Lisa

My dad died on April 5, 2020.

I'd gotten a phone call four days earlier, on April 1—no joke—from an ICU nurse, telling me that Dad was in the hospital. My brother, Dennis, and I had a brief scare, thinking Dad might have contracted COVID-19, but no, Dad had had a heart attack. (What a strange time it was that *that* news came as a relief.) And then Dad passed away due to complications from that same heart attack.

Needless to say, I had a lot of sleepless nights in April. Hard nights, when I lay in bed and stared at the ceiling in the dark. Some nights, my sleep came and went in a blink, a mere breath linking endless day to endless day, seemingly without a break in between. Other nights, my dreams were filled with monsters.

The night of April 15 was a particularly Very Bad Night, and it was taking all my energy to just try to breathe through the sobs that racked me for hours and to watch as the clock ticked steadily toward 1:00 a.m. I'd been carrying an impossible burden of grief, ~~anger,~~ anxiety, and uncertainty for what felt like years—ever since my mom died on August 21, 2018—and it was all too much.

I didn't want to do it anymore. I wanted my mom and dad back. I wanted someone else to be responsible, to make the decisions I couldn't, to face the future I didn't know what to do with.

Eventually, I managed to whisper into the dark, my words broken and raw, "I keep thinking of what Frodo said. You know—'I wish none of this had happened.'"

The bedroom was silent, and then my husband's phone lit up, Google responding to his quick search.

"'I wish the ring had never come to me,'" Tracy read to me quietly in the dark. "'I wish none of this had happened.' And then Gandalf says, 'So do all who live to see such times, but that is not for them to decide. All we have to decide is what to do with the time that is given to us.'"[13]

While I didn't magically stop crying and immediately fall into a peaceful sleep, I *was* comforted by Gandalf's words. I was able to take a breath and push back the darkness inside me for a little while.

Stories are powerful enough to save a life, and while I wasn't in danger of physically dying that night, I was in danger of losing my hope.

In a dark time, in a dark place, I reached for a line from a story as the best way to express both the scope and the nuance of how I was feeling.

And it was a passage from that same story that brought me back to the light.

> "It's like in the great stories, Mr. Frodo. The ones that really mattered. Full of darkness and danger, they were. And sometimes you didn't want to know the end. Because how could the end be happy? How could the world go back to the way it was when so much bad had happened? But in the end, it's only a passing thing, this shadow. Even darkness must pass. A new day will come. And when the sun shines, it will shine out the clearer. Those were the stories that stayed with you. That meant something, even if you were too small to understand why. But I think, Mr. Frodo, I do understand. I know now. Folk in those stories had lots of chances of turning back, only they didn't. They kept going. Because they were holding on to something."
>
> "What are we holding on to, Sam?"
>
> "That there's some good in this world, Mr. Frodo, and it's worth fighting for."[14]

You Can Do It!

How often do we turn to stories for comfort, strength, and guidance? What is it about stories that make them powerful enough to save us?

I think it's because seeing well-developed characters striving to accomplish a goal can inspire us to do the same. When a character faces conflict and adversity, it helps show us ways to deal with the conflict and adversity we encounter. And when a story highlights a powerful symbol, it can remind us to find meaning in our own lives.

Ultimately, however, I think stories are powerful because stories give us hope. They teach us "You can do it!" Stories are powerful, and as storytellers, we are in a unique position to wield that power on behalf of ourselves and on behalf of those who need hope.

And isn't that why we write? Why we tell stories? We hope to share part of ourselves, some truth that we have learned that could maybe help someone else. We hope to entertain, to enlighten, to uplift.

I hope you never underestimate the power of Story—of *your* Story.

Chapter 3
Voice: Making Your Manuscript Sing

I suspect you picked up this book because you have a story you want to tell, and you wanted to learn how to tell it better, stronger, louder.

Good.

We need that story—we need *your* story.

We need *your voice.*

As an editor, I'm often asked what I look for in a query letter or a manuscript. What is that secret, magical ingredient that turns a submission from a *maybe* to a *yes*? While there are many answers to that question, for me, it often comes down to *voice.*

I'm looking for a voice that has something to say and knows how to say it clearly and compellingly. I'm looking for a voice that demands my attention. Those voices often end up telling the stories that I am most drawn to, the stories that stick with me the longest.

Story Time with Lisa

The Dark Tower series by Steven King is seven books (or eight, depending on how you count), and it tells the story of Roland Deschain, the gunslinger, who's questing for the Dark Tower that stands at the center of the universe, the place where all stories are born, where all universes connect. Roland must reach the Tower and protect it before it falls to the man in black.

The Gunslinger, book one, was published in 1982, and book two followed in 1987. Book three released in 1991, and that's when I first became aware of the series.

I was working at a bookstore to pay for college, and I remember how many people would come into the store with a desperate, wild look in their eyes, begging to know when book four of the Dark Tower series was coming out. I would dutifully look it up on the store's system and say, "I'm sorry; there doesn't appear to be any information." This was seven years before Google was invented, so information was sparse. But I remember vowing that as interesting as I thought the story sounded, I would not pick up the series until book four was published. I knew book three ended on a really intense cliffhanger, and I did not want to become one of these same rabid fans haunting my bookstore.

My vow didn't last long. My friend, Tracy, was interested in the series, so he read the first three books and said they were amazing. I caved. Then I, too, was desperate for book four.

Six years later, book four was released, and it was exactly what I had hoped and dreamed it could be.

Then Stephen King got hit by a van and almost died.

I'm not proud of it, but my immediate worry was for Roland and the Tower because if the author died, who would finish the story?

I think King might have felt the same way because after he recovered, which took some time, he sat down and wrote books five, six, and seven in quick succession.

By then, Tracy and I were married, and when book seven came out in 2004, we bought two copies because we knew we couldn't wait for the other one to finish the book. Reading it simultaneously was tricky because sometimes he would be ahead and gasp at a plot point, and sometimes I would be ahead and gasp at a plot point, but we both reached the end near the same time.

And then something interesting happened.

At the end of the story, after all the other characters in the book found their resolution—some good, some bad, some unexpected, some not—and Roland was standing outside the door of the Dark Tower, Stephen King, the author, addressed the reader directly.

And he said this:

> I've told my tale all the way to the end, and am satisfied. . . . [But] you say you want to know how it all comes out. You say you want to follow Roland into the Tower; you say that is what you paid your money for, the show you came to see.
>
> I hope most of you know better. *Want* better. I hope you came to hear the tale, and not just munch your way through the pages to the ending. For an ending, you only have to turn to the last page and see what is there writ upon. But endings are heartless. . . .
>
> And so, my dear Constant Reader, I tell you this: You can stop here. . . .
>
> Should you go on, you will surely be disappointed, perhaps even heartbroken. . . .
>
> Would you still?[1]

Tracy turned the page so fast he practically got paper cuts.

I sat and looked at that question for a good forty-five minutes.

Because, you see, King had warned me once before at the end of *Black House* that if I continued reading, I might be unhappy. I had ignored his words, and I had been unhappy, so I took this warning seriously.

When I finally decided to turn the page, it was for the simple reason that I wanted to hear the ending of the story, good or bad, from Stephen King. I didn't want Tracy to retell it to me; I didn't want to be out and about and overhear some people saying, "Can you believe the ending of the Dark Tower?" I didn't want to hear the conclusion of this epic masterpiece from anybody other than the author.

I wanted to hear it in Stephen King's voice.

I wanted to enjoy King's final descriptions of the Tower and of Roland. I wanted to have all my senses engaged through King's skillful similes and metaphors. I wanted him to direct my attention to both the smallest of details and the epic world he had created.

Well, I did read the story all the way to the end, and I was disappointed and heartbroken. Tracy and I argued about it—he thought it was great; I disagreed—and it took me a long time to come to terms with the ending. (And don't ever tell Tracy this, but after reflection, I think he was right. I think it was the right ending for Roland's story.)

TWO DIFFERENT KINDS OF VOICE

I suspect nearly every editor or agent can agree that we like to find books that have a good voice. But the term *voice* can be confusing because it can mean either the technical aspect of the *type* of writing—active voice versus passive voice—or the artistic aspect of the *style* of writing.

The Technical

Active and Passive Voice

As a quick summary, active voice means that the subject of the sentence is performing the action expressed by the verb. Active voice keeps your writing clear, concise, and engaging.

- The boy picked up the hitchhiker.
- The hitchhiker attacked the boy.
- The boy slammed on the brakes.
- The hitchhiker flew through the windshield.

Passive voice, on the other hand, is when the subject is being acted upon; it receives the action expressed by the verb.

- ◆ The hitchhiker was picked up by the boy.
- ◆ The boy was attacked by the hitchhiker.
- ◆ The brakes were slammed on by the boy.
- ◆ The windshield was flown through by the hitchhiker.

Overused passive voice can result in flat and uninteresting prose because the characters are not acting; they are being acted upon.

I think most of us naturally use the active voice when writing. It's what we're used to reading; it's how we're used to communicating. If you're worried you might have too much passive voice in your draft, then begin by looking for the verb structures of "to be": *am*, *are*, *been*, *is*, *was*, and *were*.

The presence of the "to be" verb *was*, however, does not necessarily mean the sentence is in passive voice; it could simply be a sentence written in past tense.

The Artistry

I hate to be the bearer of bad news, but you will probably never truly master the artistry of "voice." That's because there is no finish line when it comes to developing your voice. It will change as you do—it can even change from story to story—but the more you use it, the more confident you will be with it.

To begin with, it's important to recognize that there are already multiple voices in your story. There's the author voice, the character voice, and the editor voice, and the strongest stories are when all three are working in harmony.

Author Voice

The author's voice is what makes your writing unique; it conveys your personality and attitude, and when *voice* is combined with *style*, it can create powerful storytelling.

One of the reasons I love covers of songs is because I enjoy hearing familiar lyrics set to different styles of music. It can change the meaning and the feel of the song, and sometimes the cover is even better than the original.

In some ways, *voice* is like the lyrics—it's what you have to say—while *style* is like the melody—how you choose to say it. Twisted Sister's "We're Not Gonna Take It" hits differently when it's backed by a rock drummer compared to when it's played on a ukulele.

Or a note saying "You'll always be mine" in a swirling cursive with a heart at the end versus one with the same message but in dripping blood-red letters.

I love this short passage from Gary Provost about voice:

> This sentence has five words. Here are five more words. Five-word sentences are fine. But several together become monotonous. Listen to what is happening. The writing is getting boring. The sound of it drones. It's like a stuck record. The ear demands some variety.
>
> Now listen. I vary the sentence length, and I create music. Music. The writing sings. It has a pleasant rhythm, a lilt, a harmony. I use short sentences. And I use sentences of medium length. And sometimes, when I'm certain the reader is rested, I will engage him with a sentence of considerable length, a sentence that burns with energy and builds with all the impetus of a crescendo, the roll of the drums, the crash of the cymbals—sounds that say listen to this, it is important.[2]

I hope you read that out loud. It's an interesting experience not only to feel the words on your tongue but to hear them.

As you are working to find or strengthen your voice, don't be afraid to experiment with sentence length and sentence structure, with pacing and rhythm. It's a key part of finding your own voice.

I've learned that I like to repeat a pattern of images or use sentences with a parallel structure. For example, there is a scene in *The Hourglass Door* in which the character Leo makes a drink for Abby (one "made with a story and a song and a wish"), and for the description of Abby's experience drinking it, I deliberately structured each prepositional phrase with sensory details tied to each season of the year:

"It . . . tasted of the clear, crisp air of an autumn morning, of the velvety shadows of a winter night, of the tickling green summer grass on bare feet, of the scent of the first springtime rose."[3]

My voice was the choice of words (seasonal lyrics), and my style was to group the phrasing in such a way as to emphasize the feelings and memories that Abby would find meaningful.

Character Voice

Character voice should be the strongest voice in the story. The author may be the one writing the story, but the character is the one carrying it into the reader's heart and mind.

Part of bringing your character to life is finding their voice. We touched on that topic in chapter two (when discussing Mr. Potato Head's mouth), and here are some additional factors that could influence your character's voice:

- Age
- Gender
- Education level
- The environment where they grew up
- The environment where they currently live
- Past experiences
- Their beliefs or biases
- The things they fear
- Their family history

Naturally, character voices will be different from person to person. For example, character number one, a sixteen-year-old religious monk who has been highly educated but secluded from society, should sound different from character number two, a forty-seven-year-old mercenary who has traveled the world, killed men, and now aspires to the throne, who should also sound different from character number three, who is a twenty-year-old orphan with a particular skill with horses.

While it's common to have a story written from multiple points of view, it takes effort and skill to write from four or five POVs and still maintain distinct character voices, so be careful not to have too many voices vying for the reader's attention.

World War Z by Max Brooks is an amazing dialogue-only book. The subtitle is "An Oral History of the Zombie War," and it is a brilliant set of interviews from various people who share their stories of surviving the zombie apocalypse. The characters are from all over the world, all different ages, and all had different experiences, but as the narrative flows from interview to interview, it's always clear exactly which character is speaking, even without identification.

It may take some time and practice to fully find your character's voice. One fun way that I've utilized is to answer personality quizzes or interviews as the character. If I am writing a story in third person, I will sometimes write a short scene from my character's first-person point of view to help me hear their voice better in my own head.

Once you have found your character's voice, you can use it to shape your plot in a couple of different ways. If you are using the "scene and sequel" method (as mentioned in chapter one), for example, you can highlight your character's voice during the "sequel" half of the scene structure by what they say while reacting both emotionally and logically to the action.

Likewise, knowing what your character would say in any given situation and how they would say it means you can apply pressure to character relationships to either strengthen them or break them. Think about the different ways a character could respond to the words "I love you." They could say, "I love you too." They could be cruel and say, "I don't." They could ask, "Why?" either as a joke or as a plea for connection. Any of those reactions can change the tenor of a conversation in a heartbeat.

It's also important to note that your character voice might be very different from your personal author voice. Your character may say things or believe things that you yourself do not agree with. That's okay. It's part of the process of allowing your character to find their own life and their own voice in the story.

Editor Voice

As an editor, I can't help but leave my mark on a project, but since my job is to help strengthen the author's voice and vision and to support their choices regarding character voices, I have to make sure that my voice in the story never rises above the level of a whisper. I need to stay invisible.

Authors get all of the glory; editors get all of the blame.

That's how it should be. It's your name on the cover, not mine.

If you love a book, you might praise the characters, the setting, the style, or the plot, but when was the last time you recommended a book because there wasn't a comma splice in sight or the author's use of semicolons was sublime? But for a book that you didn't like, chances are high that you'll say, "Where was the editor? How come the editor didn't fix this before it went to print?" (I've said that myself.)

As an editor, I love finding a rough spot in the text, picking apart what the words actually say, comparing them to what that author was trying to say, and then figuring out a way to help bring them back together so the reader can understand them.

Sometimes, it's a simple word switch to clarify meaning. Other times, it's restructuring the syntax for smoother reading. But sometimes, the problem requires a full rewrite in order to get the idea across. When that happens, I will either write a suggested solution for the author's approval or I'll simply ask the author to provide new text.

Whatever path the author and I take to get the material in shape, I make sure that the author's voice carries the melody while my editor's voice can provide a quieter, lighter harmony.

TIME TO SING

Let's apply some elements of voice by using the acronym SING: be Selective, be Intense, be Notorious, be Genuine.

Be Selective

As the writer, you get to choose every detail about your story: the pacing of the plot, the setting of the story, the dialogue your characters say—the characters themselves!—the style of narration, the flow of action, the symbolism, and the themes. What you draw the reader's attention to helps support both your voice and your character's voice.

That means every single detail of your book matters, so be thoughtful and deliberate in your selections. There is, after all, a vast difference between "sunflower-yellow" and "jaundice."

Be Intense

Books are based on emotion, and a strong book can inspire strong emotions—both good and bad—in the reader. But it's hard to inspire strong emotions when you say what everyone else is saying or when you sound the same way everyone else sounds.

Writing is an emotional roller coaster, as is reading. Take us on that journey. Dive deep into your own emotions so we can follow you there and feel what you are feeling—whatever that might be.

Jeff Goins wrote, "Pay attention to how you're feeling. How do you feel when writing? Afraid? Nervous? Worried? Good. You're on the right track. If you're completely calm, then you probably aren't being vulnerable. Try writing something dangerous, something a little more you. Fear can be good. It motivates you to make your writing matter."[4]

In addition to being selective, choosing intense verbs, strong nouns, and vibrant adjectives can help make your voice stand out from the crowd.

Be Notorious

We probably all have a list of authors who are insta-buys, regardless of what the story is about. We know exactly what we are going to get with their books, and we can't wait to get more of it.

What would you like to be known for as a writer? Are you great with dialogue? Do you luxuriate in deep description? Are you a fast-paced action writer? Identify your strength, and lean into it as you write.

Jeff Goins had some additional good advice:

Jot down at least five books, articles, or blogs **you like to read**. . . . How are they alike? How are they different? What about *how* they're written intrigues you? Often what we admire is what we aspire to be. *Example: Copyblogger, Chris Brogan, Seth Godin, Ernest Hemingway, and C. S. Lewis. I like these writers, because their writing is intelligent, pithy, and poignant.*

Describe yourself in **three adjectives**. *Example: snarky, fun, and flirty.*

Does your writing reflect that?

That can help you identify your own author voice. It can also help you identify your character voice. Maybe you personally aren't snarky, fun, and flirty, but maybe your protagonist is, in which case you want to be selective and intentional about writing your character voice so that the reader, if asked to describe your character in three adjectives, would say snarky, fun, and flirty.[5]

Be Genuine

Donald Maass had this to say on the subject of voice: "To set your voice free, set your words free. Set your characters free. Most important, set your heart free. It is from the unknowable shadows of your subconscious that your stories will find their drive and from which they will draw their meaning. No one can loan that or teach you that. Your voice is your self in the story."[6]

Your voice makes your story unique. That is the whole point. It's why thousands upon thousands of new stories are published every year.

It's not that one voice is necessarily *better* than another, but I think sometimes one voice can be more *confident* than another.

Patricia Lee Gauch said, "A writer's voice is not character alone, it is not style alone; it is far more. A writer's voice, like the stroke of an artist's brush, is the thumbprint of her whole person—her idea, wit, humor, passions, rhythms."[7]

What started you on your path to being a writer or a creator? What were the seeds that were planted in your life that bloomed into the desire to make your art your career? When that first fleeting, exciting idea took root inside you, what was it you wanted to say?

That is the beginning of how to develop your voice.

It's the truth you want to share.

Now, lest you get the wrong idea, I'm not saying that every story must have a lofty *theme* or proclaim a *mission* or be classified as *significant literature*. You don't have to hit me over the head with a 2 x 4 emblazoned with "the point of the story" along its side. But I do want you to say *something*.

Perhaps it is as simple as "Entertaining people makes me happy."
Perhaps it is as personal as "We are all worthy of love."

What is it you want to say?

I'm listening.

Chapter 4

How to Write an Ending—or a Sequel—That Doesn't Disappoint

I once posted on Facebook and asked my friends this question:

Hive mind:

What are some examples of books and/or movies that had terrible endings? You know, the kinds that make you throw the book across the room. The kinds that had you frothing at the mouth.

And can you tell me what it was about the story that made you feel that way?

That single post got 579 comments, none of which were from me posting or replying to anyone. It was all from other people talking to one another.

Unsurprisingly, people have strong feelings about the endings of stories. The following examples will be subjective; your mileage may vary.

PROMISES, PROMISES

The first step to writing an ending that doesn't disappoint is to write a beginning that doesn't disappoint because the two are tied together. Whatever promises you make at the beginning must be delivered by the end. They don't have to be fulfilled in a way the reader expects, but there should be closure. There should be completion.

You cannot leave your readers' expectations unfulfilled or else they will be comment #580 on my Facebook post.

I once heard Brandon Sanderson say, "Make good promises. Then make good on those promises."[1]

Readers expect certain tropes and formulas in the genres they love, so you are making a promise to them simply by stepping into that arena. Here are a few examples.

A romance will have a meet-cute close to the beginning. There will probably be a misunderstanding somewhere along the line between the couple. There must be a kiss, and it will definitely end with "happily ever after."

In mystery, chances are high there will be a death in the story. There will be clues for the detective to examine and suspects to question. There could be a red herring or two to throw them off the trail. At the end, the criminal will be caught, and justice will be served.

For a fantasy story, bet on finding magic, probably a prophecy, and definitely the chosen-one trope. Often your hero will have a sidekick, and in the end, good will defeat evil.

An action-adventure story could include fast cars or a ticking clock as the bomb counts down. Maybe it will have a chase sequence; maybe it's a standoff. Certainly, something will blow up in an explosion.

Dramas are all about character relationships under stress. We will see trauma and tears, arguments and angst. Probably some death.

When it comes to tropes, you want to hold true to your promises but without being too predictable. That's a delicate balance. We come to a book expecting the familiar, but we still want to be surprised at how we get there. One way to do that is by having unique characters who feel fully fleshed out. We may have seen this story before but never with a character like *that*! Another bit of advice I've heard is "Give them what they want but in a way they don't expect." Part of the fun of writing is adding your personal touch to the tropes.

Consider the genre you are writing and make a list of the promises you have made to the reader. Add to the list any promises that go beyond genre expectations and are specific to your story.

Finish the following statements:

- ◆ My reader should expect . . .
- ◆ My reader should feel . . .
- ◆ My reader should think . . .

Articulating those three expectations can help ensure that you are making good promises and then delivering on those promises.

Story Time with Lisa

An example of an ending that did not work for me was the movie *La La Land*. I loved the poster because it clearly had all the trappings of a romance. It had bright colors, beautiful people, and a tagline that said, "Here's to the fools who dream."

That's me! *I* am a fool who dreams. I love a good romance. I love a good musical. I was prepared to be swept away into a world of fantasy and glitz and dreams coming true.

I left the theater angry.

The movie brought me along through the characters' relationship right up to the critical point, and then there is a time jump of five years, and our two characters are now with people we've never met before. Then the movie shows a sequence of how the characters *could* have ended up together—but just . . . didn't. Don't show me a happily ever after and then tell me it was a lie.

A couple not ending up together breaks the formula of a romance, but it's not inherently a bad way to end a story. The problem was, I felt I had been promised a romance—complete with a true happily ever after—and I felt like the movie broke that promise to me.

MAKE ME CARE ABOUT THE CHARACTERS

One of the stories mentioned more than once in my Facebook post as having a frustrating ending was the movie *Grease*, and I can understand why because at the end, Danny and Sandy have both undergone a change, but it's mostly in their wardrobe.

We want to see a character change and grow beyond letterman jackets and leather pants, but when the character changes are false or feel superficial, we're going to riot.

In the case of *Grease*, I don't know that I cared enough about the characters to care that they changed. Focusing on character relationships—and how those change and grow—can help the reader be invested in the ending.

Story Time with Lisa

Please don't hate me, but *The Return of the King* is on my list of books I didn't enjoy. (I know that might be surprising considering how many examples I've shared from the series.)

I grew up reading epic fantasy, and I devoured every book I could get my hands on. I was in the eighth grade when I figured it was time to read Tolkien's Lord of the Rings. I knew the series was a classic—the pinnacle of epic fantasy—and thus, it was my duty to read the books.

I went to my dad's bookshelf and pulled down his beautiful, second-edition hardback books, complete with a massive map that folded out from the back cover. I read *The Fellowship of the Ring*, and I read *The Two Towers*, and I read about 80 percent of *The Return of the King* until I got to the scene where Frodo says, "I'm glad to be with you, Samwise Gamgee, here at the end of all things,"[2] and I remember being so tired and so frustrated that I closed the book and thought to myself, "I'm sure they will be okay."

I didn't know how the hobbits got off Mount Doom until I saw the movie version by Peter Jackson. I didn't know about the scouring of the Shire. I didn't know about any of it because I didn't care about the characters. Now, there were reasons I felt that way back then, and I recognize that the story of Frodo and Sam matters to many people.

In truth, it matters to me now. But I fell in love with Frodo and Sam from watching the movies. As it turns out, I loved the story the way Peter Jackson told it to me more than the way Tolkien told it to me.

BUILDING UP TO THE ENDING

On March 22, 2019, *Supernatural* announced that its fifteenth season would be its last, and there was severe heartbreak and anxiety in the fandom about how the story was going to end.

That August, one of the executive producers, Eugenie Ross-Leming, was quoted on Twitter as saying, "We have a year to develop it, so each episode is a piece of the ending; it's architecturally being built. Every episode carries a piece of its finality."[3]

Whether or not you believe the writers stuck the landing for the end of the show is highly personal, but I think she makes an interesting point. Ask yourself, "What in this chapter ties directly into the climactic ending of my story?"

Is there an image you can return to and recall at the end for greater impact? Are you building and layering a specific emotion? Could it be a line or a phrase or a look that will carry more weight in the moment of crisis? Is it information that could be the key to defeating the antagonist at the end?

In *The Fantasy Fiction Formula*, Deborah Chester notes, "Every scene . . . is designed to remove the protagonist's options, one by one, until the protagonist has no choice but to face the villain in the story's climax."[4]

The try/fail cycles that your protagonist is going through during the story are, in part, to eliminate the options of what *isn't* working, so that when they reach the climactic confrontation against the antagonist, their previous failures can lead to their success.

EVERYBODY DIES!

Not only is it important to build up to the ending of your story, but it's also important to build up to the ending of a character. If you *are* going to kill off a character, make sure you plan for it, work toward it, and earn that ending with a strong emotional payoff.

Story Time with Lisa

When I was in middle school, I discovered fantasy for the first time, and pretty soon, I ended up with a copy of *Dragonlance Chronicles, Volume 1: Dragons of Autumn Twilight* by Margaret Weis and Tracy Hickman.

I remember coming to the end of the book for the first time and just sobbing.

My brother happened to walk by my bedroom at that exact moment.

"Why are you crying?" he asked.

"Flint just died!" I said.

Dennis shrugged and said, "Well, go back a few pages, and he'll be alive again."

"That's not how it works!"

You get one chance for the reader to experience the character's death for the first time, so make it count and make it memorable.

Think Like a Killer

There are three facets to a criminal investigation—motive, means, and opportunity—and figuring out the *why*, the *how*, and the *when* of killing your character can help dictate the success or failure of that death.

Motive

Why are you going to kill your character?

You don't want your character to die just for the shock value or because you are making a play for readers' tears. But you might want to court death in order to strengthen the reader's emotional investment, increase the story's stakes, or deepen character conflicts.

Readers care about characters who feel real, so as an author, highlight the positives of the character and give them specific things to love and cherish and care about. Give them big dreams to shoot for.

You can also embrace their negative qualities. Giving characters relatable flaws serves two purposes: It gives your character something to overcome, and it also makes them more real—because who among us does not have a flaw or two we are hoping to overcome?

You can also showcase the character's attitude toward change. If they are open to the idea of improvement, or if we actually see them make a noticeable, profound change, we will care more about whether they live or die.

Means

There are lots of different ways a character can die. Here are a few examples of memorable deaths from stories that have stuck with me (Spoiler Alert!):

- A natural death: Joyce Summers from *Buffy the Vampire Slayer* and Grandmother Tala from *Moana*.

- Death from old age: Ellie Fredrickson from *Up*, Charlotte from *Charlotte's Web*, and Mama "Coco" Riviera from *Coco*.
- Death by illness: Beth March from *Little Women*.
- An accidental death: Leslie Burke from *Bridge to Terabithia* and Nick "Goose" Bradshaw from *Top Gun*.
- Death from a broken heart: Old Dan and Little Ann from *Where the Red Fern Grows* and Artax from *The Neverending Story*.
- Death by a family member: Gemma Teller Morrow from *Sons of Anarchy*.
- Death by suicide: Brooks from *The Shawshank Redemption*, Hannah Baker from *13 Reasons Why*, and Neil Perry from *Dead Poets Society*.
- A noble death: Robert Neville from *I Am Legend*, John Coffey from *The Green Mile*, and River Song from *Doctor Who*.
- A noble sacrifice: Spock from *Star Trek II: The Wrath of Khan* and Yondu from *Guardians of the Galaxy 2*.
- Death in battle: Ra's al Ghul from *Batman Begins*, Shepherd Book from *Firefly*, and Heimdall from *Avengers: Infinity War*.
- Death by hubris: Walter Donovan from *Indiana Jones and the Last Crusade* and Dr. Facilier from *The Princess and the Frog*.

One quick note about Dr. Facilier's death: Disney movies are no stranger to death, but the antagonist's death rarely comes at the hand of the protagonist but rather from their own mistakes or hubris. *The Princess and the Frog* would lose some of its magical charm, after all, if Tiana had wielded the blade that killed Dr. Facilier.

- Death by a secondary character: Jabba the Hutt, who is killed by Princess Leia in *Return of the Jedi*; Count Rugen, who is killed by Inigo Montoya in *The Princess Bride*; and

Gus Fring, who is killed by Hector Salamanca in *Breaking Bad*.

◆ Death at the hands of the villain: Dean Winchester from *Supernatural*, who is killed by Metatron with an angel blade in season nine; Glenn Rhee, who is killed by Negan with a wire-wrapped baseball bat in *The Walking Dead*; and Mike Ehrmantraut, who is shot by Walter White in *Breaking Bad*.

◆ Death at the hands of the hero: the Wicked Witch of the West in *The Wizard of Oz*, Kilgrave from *Jessica Jones*, and the Alien Queen from *Aliens*.

◆ Death, then resurrection: Gandalf from the Lord of the Rings and Aslan in the Chronicles of Narnia.

Opportunity

Once you've established the motive and means, it's time to choose *when* the character is going to die. As the Player says in *Rosencrantz and Guildenstern Are Dead*: "We aim at the point where everyone who is marked for death dies."[5] Choose your opportunity wisely.

Open with Death

The quintessential example of this type of death is from *Citizen Kane*. The movie begins with a slow pan over the estate of Xanadu, eventually ending in a bedroom where a man lies dying. We see a close-up of his face and his mouth as he whispers the word "Rosebud," and then a snow globe falls from his hands, rattles down the steps, and shatters into a million pieces.

Charles Foster Kane's death is the inciting incident of the story, even though it is the last moments of his life. *Citizen Kane* is then told in flashbacks and through interviews from the reporter who is digging to separate the truth from the legend behind the life of this remarkable—and remarkably flawed—man. The question that drives the story is "What does *Rosebud* mean?"

Another reason you might want to start with death is because you need to orphan the "Chosen One." The origin story of Superman involves the destruction of an entire planet. Likewise, though we don't see James and Lily Potter die on the page, they are dead when the book opens, and Harry is the "boy who lived."[6]

You may want to start with death because it allows you to introduce the monster. When we think of *Game of Thrones*, the war between the Starks and Lannisters probably comes to mind first, but the story actually begins with the rangers beyond the Wall being hunted and killed by the White Walkers. Though we don't see "the monster" again for quite some time, we know from the beginning how dangerous they are.

You may choose to start with a death that inspires revenge—cue John Wick.

And, of course, having a death at the beginning of your mystery will pose the age-old question, "Whodunit?"

Midpoint Death

Killing a character at any of the key plot points, turns, pivots, or pinches can be a powerful way to advance the plot, increase tension, raise the stakes, or motivate a character to take further action.

We've talked about Roland the gunslinger and how his quest is to reach the Dark Tower, but first, he must capture the man in black.

Along Roland's journey, he encounters a young boy named Jake, who is not from Roland's world. Jake has no one to protect him or help him find his way home, except for Roland. Partway through the book, the gunslinger, with Jake in tow, is within striking distance of the man in black. In the ensuing action, Jake falls from the bridge, but Roland catches him at the last second. Now Roland must choose: Save Jake and let the man in black escape? Or drop Jake and continue his quest?

He drops Jake.

While Roland is the protagonist and the man in black is the antagonist, this moment reveals a crucial aspect of Roland's character. Jake's death changes how we feel about Roland and reinforces how ruthless he can be in accomplishing his goal.

End with Death

If you've earmarked a character for death at the end of the story, start subtly preparing us for it as soon as possible. Perhaps choose something symbolic to the character, which, when brought back at the moment of death, can have a greater impact.

In *Jojo Rabbit*, there are a number of shots in which we only see Rosie's red-and-white shoes. They symbolize her beauty, playfulness, and love of life. At the end, when we see her shoes hanging in midair, unmoving, we don't have to be told how she died; the shoes do it for us.

On the other hand, you may choose to end with an *unexpected* death. When Eddard Stark is beheaded at the end of *Game of Thrones*, it signals to the reader that anyone can die in the book. No amount of plot armor will protect someone simply because they are established as a primary point-of-view character. And for fans of *Firefly*, the phrase "I am a leaf on the wind"[7] is enough to bring us to tears as we mourn the unexpected death of Hoban Washburne.

Some Death Tropes to Avoid

One example of a death trope to avoid is known as "Bury Your Gays," in which a character is killed or brutalized simply because they have revealed their gender or sexual orientation to another character.[8]

Another example is known as "fridging," which is a term coined by Gail Simone in 1999 and named after the 1994 release of *Green Lantern (Volume 3)* #54, in which the title hero comes home to his apartment to find that his girlfriend has been killed by the villain and literally stuffed into a refrigerator. Thus "fridging" has come to identify the trend of using the death or other type of brutalization of a female character for the sole purpose of causing emotional trauma or cheap anger to force the male protagonist into action.[9]

Both of these kinds of deaths devalue the life of the victim and reduce them to a mere plot device instead of an actual character.

In *Avengers: Endgame*, Natasha, aka. the Black Widow, has a very dramatic and sacrificial death. She and Clint, aka. Hawkeye, are at the top of a cliff, and they know a sacrifice must be made to claim the Soul Stone required to defeat Thanos. It's either Natasha or Clint. After some discussion and a bit of a battle, Natasha is the one who makes the leap and dies at the bottom of the cliff.

An argument could be made that her death is not fridging because Black Widow's character did more for the story than merely exist to die and that she chose to sacrifice herself to save Clint's family and her fellow Avengers, but as is quoted in *The Escapist Magazine*: "It doesn't feel like a satisfying conclusion to [Natasha's story]. It sacrifices organic character work for the immediate thrill of upsetting audience expectation. It offers no insight. It just adds another line to the plot summary."[10]

Did Natasha's sacrifice change the story? In other words, how might the story have changed if Clint had been the one to die and Natasha the one to live?

After Natasha's death, Clint's role was mostly to shoot monsters beneath the Avengers complex to save the new Infinity Gauntlet. Could Natasha have done that? Yeah, probably. We'd just need to choreograph a new fight scene.

Was it worth it to kill one of the few female Avengers for dramatic effect?

SIX STEPS TO A STRONG ENDING

In *The Fantasy Fiction Formula*, Deborah Chester outlines six steps[11] to build a strong ending, and we can see all six steps in action during the ending of *Star Wars: A New Hope*.[12]

As we draw toward the climactic ending, the story establishes that the Death Star will shortly be in position to blow up Yavin, and so *step one* is to make a choice: go now or not at all.

Step two is the sacrifice. This happens when Luke Skywalker, in his X-wing, struggles to stay in the trench as the other pilots are getting blasted away, and he hears Obi-Wan Kenobi's voice say, "Use the Force, Luke."

The sacrifice, then, is this: Do you put aside the technological instrumentation of this powerful ship that is designed to help you make a one-in-a-million shot and blow up the Death Star? Will you sacrifice that and instead rely on this nebulous spiritual Force that you are not yet trained in?

Step three, acting upon the sacrifice, happens almost immediately. Luke decides to follow Obi-Wan's voice, and he pushes the button to put his equipment away.

Now comes the dark moment—*step four*—where R2-D2 is shot. Now Luke has nothing. R2-D2 can't help. His equipment is no longer at his fingertips. The other pilots have been destroyed or pulled away. It's up to him to make the shot to blow up the Death Star.

But then—*step five*—the reversal! Just as it appears that Luke will be shot down, Han Solo swoops in with the Millennium Falcon to rescue him. When Han says, "You're all clear, kid! Now, let's blow this thing and go home!" we feel a surge of hope.

The Death Star blows up, and Luke is rewarded—*step six*—with the promise that "the Force will be with you always," and Darth Vader is punished, and we see his ship spiraling out into space.

Cue end credits.

BUT WAIT! I'M WRITING A SERIES!

Great! Go for it! Sometimes it takes a duology, a trilogy, a saga, or a series to tell the whole story.

Writing your first book can feel like magic, stars descending from the heavens. It can be as cozy as a kitten sleeping on a stack of books in a quiet library. It's feeling like you and your muse will be best friends forever. You get to play with your characters, experiment with new storylines, introduce a new world, and build to an exciting cliffhanger. Hooray!

And by the time you get to book three, your story is running at full speed and heading toward an epic conclusion in which everything gets resolved. Hooray!

But what about book two? It's a weird in-between space where characters need to demonstrate growth but not grow too much, where the plot needs to continue but not conclude, and where the stakes need to be higher than book one but not as high as book three.

Writing a sequel can feel like an overwhelming sense of "I have no idea what I'm doing," with the Grim Reaper looming behind you, holding a scythe and pointing to a deadline. By the time you're elbow-deep into the sequel, it's easy to relate to the meme of a dog sitting in a burning room, saying, "This is fine."

Moving on Up!

When writing a series, it's helpful to stop thinking horizontally and start thinking vertically. If book one is about establishment, and book three is about execution, then book two is about elevation. But it's not a straight shot to the top; it's more like a spiral going onward and upward.

I like to move my characters forward using Joseph Campbell's Hero's Journey. While there are seventeen official stages[13] to the plot structure, a quick shorthand can simplify it to five steps.

- ◆ **Adventure** moves your character from the call to adventure to the first threshold.

- **Adversity** covers the entrance into the unknown world, meeting the mentor, and walking the road of challenges and temptations.
- **Abyss** is the character's death and rebirth.
- **Atonement** is when the character, reborn and transformed, begins their journey to wholeness.
- **Acceptance** is the character's return from the unknown to the known world along with the boon.

When writing a series, remember that not all of your characters will start the Hero's Journey at the same time, but getting them all to their individual finish lines at the same time can make for a thrilling ending.

Let's look once again at a classic: *Star Wars*.

In *A New Hope*, Luke Skywalker is answering the call to adventure. Han Solo, however, is already wading through the adversity phase of his character journey. And Obi-Wan Kenobi is all the way on the other side of the cycle, offering atonement.

In *The Empire Strikes Back*, Luke is now wading through adversity, Han Solo is facing the abyss by being frozen in carbonite, and Leia is answering the call to adventure.

In *Return of the Jedi*, Luke is achieving reconciliation as he comes face-to-face with Darth Vader, Han Solo is emerging from the abyss and beginning his transformation, and Anakin Skywalker has been redeemed, though he is unable to return to the world he had once left behind.

Ask three simple questions for each character in each book.

1. Which phase is this character in when they start their journey?
2. Which phase should they be in when they end?
3. What is the next step of their journey?

If they are repeating all or part of the cycle from adventure to acceptance, what knowledge or skill do they have now that they didn't before? Which characters can you advance along their journey more quickly, and which characters can you delay along the way for dramatic purposes?

Elevate, Broaden, Narrow, and Expand

In addition to thinking vertically, writing a sequel or a series also requires you to think multidimensionally in four specific ways.

Elevate the threat. The Harry Potter series is an example of how a hero and a villain can take multiple steps along parallel paths to help elevate the threats. As Voldemort grows in strength and power from book to book, so does Harry.

- Book 1: Harry versus Professor Quirrell.
- Book 2: Harry versus Tom Riddle via the diary.
- Book 3: Harry versus the Dementors.
- Book 4: Harry versus Barty Crouch Jr. and the Death Eaters.
- Book 5: Harry versus Dolores Umbridge in the Ministry of Magic.
- Book 6: Harry versus Draco and Snape (and dealing with Dumbledore's death).
- Book 7: Harry versus Voldemort, in person.

To elevate the threat in your own story, make a list of your try/fail cycles in book one, and then make a list of what your character learned from those cycles. How can you challenge the character's new knowledge in book two? What new goals did your protagonist set at the end of book one? What about your antagonist's goals?

You can also elevate the threat by flipping it so that what was an external threat is now internal, or vice versa.

Broaden the goals. The main goal in the Lord of the Rings is to destroy the One Ring, but each individual book has additional, and sometimes unexpected, goals. Along the way to Mount Doom, the Fellowship must also win the battle of Helm's Deep, reclaim the throne of Gondor, and stop Saruman, to name a few.

Narrow the motivation. As Ironman, Tony Stark establishes a motivation that narrows from "I will do this for the world" to "I will do this for the ones I love" to "I will do this because I'm the only one who can."

Likewise, an antagonist such as Jafar in *Aladdin* changes his motivation from "I will destroy the world" to "I will destroy the hero's loved ones" to "I will destroy the hero specifically."

Expand the structure. Whether you look at story structure on a chapter level, a book level, or a series level, you can create synchronicity between plot points and thematic elements. What symbols or themes from book one can you continue to develop in book two? What lines of dialogue can you repeat in a new context? What actions can a character take that carries new meaning? What plot points can you align for greater effect? For example, character one might be experiencing a try/fail cycle that lines up exactly with character two's midpoint pivot.

You can incorporate any or all of these four elements within a single book as you move your protagonist to the climax or from book to book as part of an ongoing series.

END ON A HIGH NOTE

The day after I posted on Facebook, asking for stories with bad endings, I asked my friends to tell me about the books that had endings they loved. To my surprise, that post had very little engagement, and most of the responses were along the lines of, "I don't remember exactly how it ended, but I remember I loved it."

I once heard Tracy Hickman say, "Books are the souvenirs of the journey,"[14] and I think that is true. My library is filled with books that I might never reread, but I can't bear to part with them because I remember how I felt after reading them.

Endings can make or break your book—as well as how your reader feels about the story as a whole—so take the time to end on a high note.

THAT'S A WRAP!

When it comes to endings, you want them to be psychologically fulfilling, dramatically thrilling, and emotionally satisfying. You need to bring the conflict to a showdown, tie off the remaining subplots, resolve your primary story question, and prove the protagonist worthy of reward and the antagonist deserving of failure or justice.

Easy, right?

Well, ask yourself this:

* Did you answer your primary story question?
* Did your hero solve the problem themself?
* Did your hero stay true to their motivations and goals?
* Did you show evidence of character growth?
* Did you earn the emotional catharsis honestly?
* Did you reward the just and punish the unjust?
* Did you provide resolution?

If you answered yes to any one of these questions, congratulations, you have written an ending that doesn't disappoint.

Chapter 5
Breaking Through Writer's Block

Is writer's block real?

Yes!

Being creative on demand can be a challenge. You may feel stuck in your story for any number of real, valid reasons. Perhaps your characters are underdeveloped. Maybe your plot is sluggish, but you don't know why. It could be that your idea is not robust enough to withstand the pressure of development. And maybe you just honestly don't know what happens next.

On the flip side, sometimes writer's block is simply a handy excuse for procrastination. It becomes a self-fulfilling prophecy: you don't write because you *can't* write, and you can't write because you *don't* write.

When I feel stuck in a story, I take a deep breath and remind myself that this is simply an opportunity to solve the problem creatively.

I am a creative person. I like solving problems. And when I encounter writer's block, it usually means there is a problem with the story, character, plot, or idea. Rather than saying, "There's nothing I can do; I have writer's block," I take the power back and say, "I'm going to solve this problem."

The best part is that it doesn't have to be the right solution, or even a good solution. I just need to come up with one idea that can get me back on track. Here are some methods I have used to help me break through the block.

Step Back

We talked about how plot needs forward momentum, and one way to think about that is that small problems will lead to larger problems, larger problems will lead to confrontations, and confrontations will lead to character growth, and character growth makes for interesting reading.

If you're stuck, take a few steps back to see if you can identify if you have problems that are not leading to solutions or if you have confrontations that are not leading to growth, and try to change the focus of the scene to get your story back on track.

Skip It

Sometimes you just have to get out of your own way, sit down, and write a path through it or around it or over it. After all, there's no rule that says you have to write your story chronologically. If you run into a roadblock at one point in your story, you can skip that part. I won't tell anyone.

My first drafts are littered with bracketed notes that say "Insert something cool here" or "Look this up later" or "This doesn't work. Rewrite later." I may not know what words will end up there, but I do know that if I stop writing, I'll risk derailing my momentum and focus. It's much easier to skip the tricky bit and write the exciting stuff.

Change Where You Write

Sometimes changing where you write is enough to kick you into a different gear. If you write at your kitchen table, maybe write upstairs in the bedroom. If you write at the library, maybe try writing at Starbucks. Sometimes a change of scenery can change your viewpoint.

Change How You Write

If you have written on your computer up to this point, try writing the next chapter with a ballpoint pen and lined paper. The slower pace of writing by hand might unlock the story in a way that helps you get through the troubling spot, or it might uncover an idea you hadn't thought of before.

Set a Deadline

There is nothing like a contractually obligated deadline to force you to be creative. Even if you don't have a contract, you can still set a timer and do writing sprints. The idea is to take yourself out of the equation and focus on doing the task at hand.

Story Time with Lisa

It took me about eight months to write the first draft of *The Hourglass Door*, and while the pages were still hot from the printer, my publisher, Chris, said, "Great! Where's book two?"

I thought, *Can't I have one moment to enjoy having turned in the first book?*

But he was right. I had signed a contract for the trilogy, and if I wanted book two to release a year after book one, and if we were going to do advance reading copies (ARCs), I needed to turn in *The Golden Spiral*, not in eight months but in four.

I had to figure out how to write the same number of words in half the time.

I had about a twenty-minute train ride into my office every day, so I started writing in twenty-minute sprints, twice a day, to and from work. I would sit down, write nonstop for the length of my commute, then go to work, and on the way home, I'd write nonstop for another twenty minutes.

On Saturdays, I'd take all those little paragraphs I'd churned out in my handful of minutes during the week and spend eight or nine hours finishing a chapter, outlining the next one, and getting ready for the next week's train rides.

But writing toward a deadline meant I couldn't afford to listen to the voice in my head that said, "Don't do that." I didn't have time to come up with a better idea. I had to get the words down.

Which is how I essentially wrote 100,000 words in twenty-minute increments in four months.

Raise the Stakes

It's possible you're stuck in your story because nothing compelling enough is happening to force your characters into action.

Simply blow something up in the story. This could be either physical or emotional. It could be a startling revelation—a secret finally revealed, a truth finally told. It could also be an actual bomb going off. If you can introduce an action, your characters will be forced to react, to make decisions, and to move the story forward.

Story Time with Lisa

I was writing book three in my trilogy, *The Forgotten Locket*, and I was stuck. I told my writing group I didn't have any pages to share that week, but I wanted everybody to come up with ten things they thought could happen at the end of the book. "What's the worst thing that could happen in my story?" I asked. "Bring me your answers."

And my writing group delivered. They had wild ideas, great ideas, and even some bad ideas, but they all helped kick-start my creativity and helped me see a path through the story.

When I came home, my husband asked, "How was group?"

"It was great."

"Which idea are you going to do?"

"I'm gonna do all of them!"

From that point on, if I got stuck, I would look at the scene and say, "What's the worst thing that could happen in this moment right now?" and then I would write that.

And because I was writing the last book of the series, I kept telling myself, "What am I waiting for? Why am I holding back? I don't have to play it safe."

Embrace the Unexpected

I like outlining my stories. I like knowing where the story is going, and how I'm going to get there. But sometimes stories have a mind of their own, and when they stop being obedient to an outline, writer's block can set in.

When that happens, I think to myself: *Zombies.*

Story Time with Lisa

I struggled with writer's block nearly the entire time I was writing *The Forgotten Locket*. I had used up all my paid leave from work trying to finish it. I missed my deadline twice. I had written and then thrown away about 30,000 words that didn't work. I was very stressed.

Then Dennis helpfully said, "You know what your story needs? A zombie apocalypse. No one will expect a zombie apocalypse at the end of your young adult love story."

He was right, of course. Nobody would've expected a zombie apocalypse instead of the "happily ever after" I was aiming for. But

I also knew I didn't want one. Whenever I paused or stopped or ran into a dead end, I would think, "Well, if I can't come up with a good idea, I'm gonna have to write a zombie apocalypse." Just the idea of it gave me the inspiration to keep moving forward.

For most of that book, I felt the hot breath of zombies on my neck and could hear their shuffling footsteps right behind me. I just kept trying to write faster than they were moving because I was *not* going to put zombies in my book.

I still wasn't finished with my draft when my birthday arrived, so my brother wrote the first draft of the end of the story for me as a present:

> Dante leaned in close to Abby, cradling her in his arms.
>
> "Oh, Dante," she sighed. "I can't believe our love story has come to such a wonderful end."
>
> "I know, right?" Dante said. "Who would have guessed it would have happened like that?"
>
> "It was pretty exciting," Abby said. "But also, like, super romantic and stuff."
>
> Remember that kiss from the end of *The Princess Bride*? Well, that's totally how Abby and Dante kissed, only way better.
>
> "Tell me what you love most about me." Abby smiled as she updated her Facebook status to "Dating Dante LOL!"
>
> Dante grinned really evil and creepy-like, sort of like Heath Ledger as the Joker.
>
> "I think the thing I love most about you," he said, licking his lips hungrily, "are your BRAAAIIIINS!!"
>
> Abby never saw it coming.
>
> The end.[1]

The idea of "embracing the unexpected" is similar to "raising the stakes," but I think they have some differences. When I'm looking to raise the stakes, I might lean into ideas that are absurd or unexpected in order to create new scenarios and conflicts, but the idea behind embracing "zombies" is that I'm actively avoiding a scenario I don't want to write. Either way, I find myself adding words to my story, which is the best way to break through writer's block.

EMBRACE YOUR POWER

"Adding words" is also at the heart of the idea of writing fearless. When you are faced with a blank page, *add some words*. When you want to get to know your characters better, *add some words about them*. When you start to sink into the swampy middle of your story, *add some words to build a bridge to get you out*.

Remember, they don't have to be the best words you've ever written. Embrace your ability to write all kinds of words—both silly and smart words—and see how quickly you can fill up your pages.

EDIT SMART

Chapter 6
Editing: Hang on to Your Hats and Glasses!

Spoiler Alert! Writing and editing are two different tasks. They use different parts of your brain, and they have different goals, which means you shouldn't try to do both at the same time.

As an author, you are attempting to transmit your story, idea, or message out of your head and into the reader's mind. To that end, you have worked hard on developing your characters. You have structured your plot and kept track of your pacing. You've worked to streamline your prose. You've made efforts to strengthen your voice. You've attempted to fix the basic errors in grammar, spelling, and punctuation, even if you've only used your computer's spell check or a program like Grammarly or PerfectIt. Hopefully, you've kept an eye on your details, ensuring their consistency throughout the course of the story (if your character begins with green eyes, they should end with green eyes).

As with writing, editing is about clarity, creativity, communication, and connection. But the editor's job is not to write—or rewrite—your book. It's to help you successfully and seamlessly bridge the gap between you and the reader through thorough developmental editing and precise copyediting.

As an editor, I have a responsibility to both the book and the author. When it comes to the book, my job is to double-check an author's work by reviewing the plot structure, streamlining the prose, preserving the author's voice, delving into the deep mysteries of grammar and spelling and punctuation, and keeping the story elements consistent.

My responsibility to the author includes offering support, helping to brainstorm ideas, answering questions about the publishing process, and being a resource and a teammate and, hopefully, a friend. I may also challenge an author to come up with a better metaphor, find a different description, make a character's insult more cutting, add more heat to a kiss, or heighten the stakes by making them more personal.

TERMINOLOGY

In general, editing is a top-down process of clearing away the larger trees, then the smaller trees, then the boulders, then the medium-sized rocks, then the little pebbles until you reach smooth ground, ready for planting (i.e., publishing). When we talk about editing, there are several different kinds, so it's important to know the terminology.

Developmental editing—sometimes called "content editing" or "substantive editing"—is the 30,000-foot-view above the story. It's where you're looking at plot structure, character arc, thematic development, and pacing issues. It's the time to identify large elements that don't need to be there as well as identify plot holes or make suggestions of what should be there that could help strengthen the story.

It's important to finalize developmental edits before undertaking copyedits because if you spend a lot of time copyediting a particular chapter, making sure all the commas are correct, only to discover later that you need to cut that entire chapter, you have expended a lot of effort, time, and possibly money fixing pages that ended up on the cutting room floor.

The second level of editing is sometimes called line editing or **copyediting**, and that is where an editor looks at the nuts and bolts of grammar, spelling, and punctuation. Line by line, word by word, character by character, we make sure every aspect is exact according to the dictionary, *The Chicago Manual of Style*, the publishing house's style guide, and even sometimes according to the author's preference and internal story consistency. (We'll talk more about copyediting in chapter seven.)

The third level is **proofreading**, which happens once the copyedited manuscript has been typeset into "proofs." At that stage of the process, a design has been applied to the material, the page numbers and running heads have been placed correctly, the fonts have been chosen, the margins have been adjusted, any visual elements have been applied, and the manuscript now, for the first time, looks like a book. Those proofs are then sent to a proofreader, who looks for errors in the design and typography. They may also find errors in the text, but those mistakes should ideally be the small pebbles of missing or misspelled words and perhaps a few misplaced punctuation marks.

EDITING FOR VOICE

Editing can be as creative, artistic, and personal as writing can be, and I often remind myself that "the best idea wins," even if it's not mine. I may edit a clunky sentence, and the author may come back and change it even further, which is perfectly fine. The goal, after all, is to get the best sentence possible for the reader.

One of the hardest tasks I do is edit for voice, because every author's voice is different. But what does that look like?

Word Choice

While I'm editing, I'm constantly asking myself, "Will this change make it *right* or just *different*?" And the follow-up question is, "Even if it is technically *right*, is it right for the author's voice and for this story?"

I have worked with an author who tends to focus the character's body language on eyes and hands. There is a lot of "looking" and "glancing" and "putting her hand on his arm" and "turning around." I will admit, I take out as much of the repetition as I can, but I also leave several of those instances in because that is part of the author's voice. It's part of what makes her books uniquely *hers*.

Story Time with Lisa

I was only a few years into my career when I was assigned to edit a historical novel set during the American Revolutionary War. The author had already written two books in the series, but his previous editor had a scheduling conflict, so the project came to me. I was both excited and terrified. This would be the first big project I would be in charge of, and I wanted to do my best work.

But because I was young, it meant I was also trying too hard; I was doing too much.

I remember a passage where the author was describing a breakfast scene. The characters had gathered around the table to enjoy jam and bread. Whether it was instinct or bias or because I was trying to prove that I knew what I was doing, I changed it to "bread and jam." (I suspect it stemmed from all the times I'd read *Bread and Jam for Francis* by Russell Hoban as a child.)

I didn't think much of the edit until the author sent it back marked "stet," meaning to leave the original text.

I'll admit I was mad. How dare the author question my judgment? I was *The Editor*. But after I calmed down, I was able to take a step back and recognize that there was nothing wrong with "jam and bread." All the words were spelled correctly, they were used appropriately, and they communicated the idea with clarity. The fact that I thought it didn't "sound right" was not a good enough reason to change it.

Now when I'm editing, I sometimes have a "bread and jam" check, in which I will ask myself: Am I changing this because it's actually wrong and needs to be fixed, or am I changing it because it's not how I would have done it?

Looking back now, I am grateful for having learned an extremely valuable lesson, even if at the time, it was a struggle.

Consistency

Editing for voice might also look like "consistency." If an author prefers short sentences and I combine them into a sentence that is eighty words long . . . well, that edit is going to stand out for all the wrong reasons.

Likewise, perhaps the author likes to use adjectives or metaphors. Perhaps they enjoy employing alliteration or assonance for dramatic effect. Perhaps they like to repeat words or ideas in threes—like I just did here.

Whatever the author's style and voice, my job is to be aware of it and then keep that tone and flow consistent throughout the book.

Rewriting

Sometimes, editing for voice requires rewriting. If I come across a passage that needs substantial work, I'll either send it back to the author to fix, or I'll take a crack at it and then leave the author a question asking if my suggestion works or if they would like to revise it further.

Story Time with Lisa

Several years ago, I got to edit a nonfiction book that my brother had written. (Finally, I could boss him around!)

While working on the manuscript, I took out three or four paragraphs and replaced them with two or three sentences. Because I knew what he was trying to say and how he would have said it, I felt confident that I could fix the problem the way he would have. Later, after the book was out, Dennis mentioned the section that I had rewritten for him and said, "Man, this is such a great line. I didn't know I was such a great writer."

"Yeah," I agreed. "*I* wrote that line."

Ultimately, "editing for voice" looks like building a good relationship with an author so that I know how best to help them tell their story.

SELF-EDITING

While the editor works hand in hand with the author to make their words shine, there are some tasks an author can do to help make the editing process work better too.

Step one: wait. When you are done writing, put the manuscript aside. Tuck it into a drawer or a designated folder on your computer, and don't look at it for a while. Distance is a valuable tool because when a story has been poured hot from your brain onto the page, chances are high that you'll miss some errors if you try to edit it right away. Your brain knows what it expects to see on the page, so it will helpfully fill in missing words and correct misspellings. Your eyes may gloss over problems as you read. By giving yourself distance and time, you'll be able to be more objective about the strengths and weaknesses of your own work when you come back to it.

When you do come back to it, you'll want to bring along some helpful hats and glasses.

Wear the Right Hat

When it comes time to start editing, I want you to grab the right hat. Up until now, you've been wearing your writer hat while you've brainstormed ideas, characters, dialogue, world-building, and plot twists. But before you swap out your writer hat for your editor hat, I want you to wear the hat of the *reader*. It's the same hat I wear when I start a developmental edit.

Along with the hat, you'll want to gather your reading tools. Perhaps you like to print the manuscript, sit in a comfy chair, and write directly on the pages with a red pen. Or you may choose to leave notes for yourself using the comment function in Word. Either way, it's important to note your reaction the minute you have it.

When I'm reading a manuscript for the first time, I am highly attuned to my thoughts and emotions. If I think something is funny, I'll make a note. If I am confused by a character's behavior, I'll make a note. That way, when I'm sending my editorial notes to the author, they will know exactly, with pinpoint precision, where a problem might have its roots.

In the case of a mystery, once I have a suspicion of who the murderer is, I'll leave a note. If I figured it out too soon, then the author knows they need to add more clues, more red herrings, and more MacGuffins to throw me off track again.

While you are reading, I would encourage you to have a dedicated space where you can be creative and a different dedicated space where you can be critical. When I was writing *The Hourglass Door*, I would sit on the couch in my family room. But if I sat in that same spot when I was trying to edit, I found it harder to be objective because I was in my creative space.

When I do developmental reading and edits, I also like to read uninterrupted as much as possible. Swallowing the book in one big gulp helps me see the shape and scope of the entire story, and I can more easily follow the thematic threads the author is weaving into the words. I can keep track of the story arcs to make sure the characters are growing and changing appropriately. It also helps me see what is missing. An often-underappreciated skill of a good editor is that they can not only fix what's there, but they can also fix what's *not* there and articulate what *should* be there in order to make the story better and stronger.

Much like a doctor whose first rule is "do no harm," editors should fix what is wrong but not break what is right.

Wear the Right Glasses

While you are reading through the manuscript, marking the high-level issues, take time to switch out your glasses and look for specific elements as well. You may wish to do this on separate passes so you can focus on each section in turn.

Rose-Colored Glasses. In addition to making notes of your emotional and intellectual reactions to the story, put on a pair of rose-colored glasses and mark the language you love. Find instances of beautiful imagery, smart dialogue, and vivid action. Note your favorite characters and cheer for them. Identify strong metaphors. Keeping track of the words you love, the words you feel add strength to your story, also gives you a list of what you don't have to fix because they're not broken.

Blackout Sunglasses. There are plenty of problems I ignore on a first-pass developmental edit, so I wear a pair of blackout sunglasses to help me ignore the small errors of misspelled or missing words, misplaced commas, and isolated instances of clunky syntax. I know I'm going to fix them later, during a copyedit pass, so for now, I focus on the other sets of glasses. (Having said that, sometimes I can't help myself, and I'll fix it when I see it.)

Magnifying Lenses. The third pair of glasses are the lenses that help you look for story elements to fix. These can include consistency issues, plot holes, and needless instances of repetition, both in dialogue and narration. You want to find places where a point of view or verb tense has shifted. Those are pretty big problems that will need to be fixed.

Safety Goggles. Strengthening your manuscript might require some heavy rebuilding and renovation, so make sure you've got your safety goggles on as you dig deep into finding ways to improve your own voice or your characters' unique voices. You may find spots where your theme could be boosted. Perhaps your characters need a better, deeper backstory. You may want to increase the conflict by strengthening or breaking relationships.

EDITING AND REVISING FOR PLOT, CHARACTER, AND THEME

Now that you've identified some issues that need to be fixed or strengthened, take off your hat and glasses, and let's dig deeper into plot, character, and theme and ask some questions that might help during your next revision pass.

Look at Your Plot

Chances are your story has strayed from your original outline. That's normal. But now that the story is written, do you still have a solid structure? To find out, it might be helpful to build a reverse outline. There are two ways to do that. One way is to reuse the same plot structure that you developed at the start of the project and make sure the story beats still hit in the right spots. Another way is to use a *different* plot structure to see if looking at the story through a new lens reveals any weak spots or missing plot points.

For example, I like to draw the seven-point arc structure multiple times and fill in each one with the key elements of plot for each character as well as for their external and internal goals. But I could also pour my story into the "Save the Cat" method to see what changes—if anything.

You can also look at your story chapter by chapter and, for each one, answer the following questions:

- Who is the point-of-view character?
- What new information do they learn?
- What action do they take?
- How does this chapter move the plot forward?

That should give you a solid summary of your story that you can use to check for pacing and flow—and maybe even as a springboard for your query letter. (More about those in chapter nine.)

Look at Your Character Arcs

If your book has a large cast of characters, make a chart of which character is the POV of which chapter so you can see at a glance if the pacing is flowing evenly. As you move back and forth among various points of view, the chart can also help you see if a particular point-of-view character is dominating the narrative or if you need to strengthen a different point of view to provide balance.

Along with the character chart, it can be helpful to summarize the action of what happens in each chapter. For example, you might summarize chapter two as: "Protagonist prepares to take final test. Learns more about world history. Description of the building." Once you've done that for every chapter of a particular character's point of view, you can read through the summarized action of the character's arc and development based solely on what's actually in your book.

Likewise, you can analyze character arcs with this series of questions:

- Where did the character begin?
- What are the events that triggered their change?
- Is there a logical progression to the character's development?
- Are there any gaps in the character's timeline?
- Where does the character end up?

Look at Your Themes

Identify the symbols you've used that are helping to establish the theme of your book. Are there areas in the manuscript where you can strengthen those themes through dialogue or action?

Often themes can grow out of familiar plot tropes. For example, some tropes could include "overcoming the monster," "rags to riches," "the quest," "voyage and return," "comedy," "tragedy," or "rebirth." Within each of those tropes could be elements that you could turn into a symbol.

What might "overcoming the monster" look like in a contemporary romance? It's unlikely to be a literal monster or a boogeyman under the bed, but if the "monster" your heroine is trying to overcome is the fear of rejection, then perhaps you draw the reader's attention to the sound of doors closing throughout the story, and then, when she overcomes that fear, the doors in her life begin to open.

Another way to find and strengthen themes and symbols is by looking at the places where you use sensory imagery or language: sight, sound, smell, taste, and touch. I was working with a first-time author and recommended that he include three sensory images in every chapter. That is not a hard-and-fast rule, of course—I made it up on the spot—but my goal wasn't to force him to focus on the number but rather to help him be conscious of the need for sensory language in the story because sensory images are often folded into metaphors and similes, and metaphors and similes help develop theme.

A metaphor is a word or phrase denoting an object or idea that is used in place of another to suggest a likeness, while a simile compares two unlike things and is often introduced by the words "like" or "as." It's the difference between saying, "She was a bird," and, "She was like a bird." Personally, I think similes are easier to use than metaphors, but both tools can be incredibly useful.

You can also use physical objects to illustrate an intangible concept or emotion. A character who has a short temper might wear a bright-red shirt. Or you might repeat symbolic motifs to establish the theme. For example, you might use imagery of birds associated with a character who longs for freedom.

As I was helping Dennis get started on a new novel, I challenged him to find an object in his first chapter that he could use as a symbol throughout the story. He had written a scene about a flight attendant feeling out of place and unsure of herself as she started her first day of work on a new airline.

I suggested the luggage on the plane could be symbolic. We talked about the main character's suitcase that she would bring on board with her and what it might mean to her. What could it embody? Why was it important for her to be a flight attendant? As we talked through some possible answers, he discovered some great insights into her as a character and into her backstory and her motivations. He figured out she was frustrated that her route wasn't taking her to places like France, Japan, or Australia. She was flying to Boise, Idaho, and Reno, Nevada—short hops from where she lived in Las Vegas. We talked about how perhaps her suitcase could be covered in stickers of all the places she *wished* she could go. Or conversely, perhaps her suitcase didn't have any decorations on it at all because she hadn't been anywhere yet.

Almost anything in your book can be a symbol that supports a theme once you connect it to your characters' wants or dreams or needs.

LOOK, LISTEN, AND SHARE

In the same way that you want time between writing the manuscript and editing it, you also want some time between editing the manuscript and sharing it with others. Here are a couple more tips to help that process.

Change the Look

Standard manuscript submission format is Times New Roman font, 12-point type, double-spaced, with one-inch margins. However, once I'm done reading a manuscript and I'm ready to put on my editor's hat, I change the font to Verdana, which is a sans serif font designed for the screen. It's slightly larger than Times New Roman, and when I magnify my screen to 150 percent or 180 percent, it makes it easier on my eyes.

Changing the font also changes how I approach the material. I write in Times New Roman, but I edit in Verdana, and when I make the switch, that visual cue tells me, "Don't think about this text as a writer. Think about this text as an editor." That helps me be more analytical and approach the story more objectively.

Read It Out Loud

I also strongly recommend that you read your manuscript once on paper and once out loud. It's a different experience looking at the words on a computer screen versus when you look at them on paper. I'm always surprised at how many mistakes I see that I would have otherwise missed when the manuscript is printed out. Likewise, when you read your manuscript out loud or have the computer read it to you, it's easier to hear clunky sentences that could use another refinement pass. You'll find the missing words when you trip over where they should be. You'll hear the repetition that perhaps your eyes have glossed over.

Share Your Story

Fresh eyes are the best eyes to find fresh mistakes, which is why having alpha readers, beta readers, and critique partners can be so helpful. Not only can you gather valuable feedback on your own story, but it also gives you a chance to hone your own analytical and editing skills. Somehow, it's always easier to see problems in other people's work, and being able to identify and articulate the kinds of errors you find in other people's manuscripts can help you when you look for those same errors in your own. Writing groups can also hold you accountable for your goals and deadlines.

Story Time with Lisa

I had been working as an editor for about a decade when my friend and coworker Tony mentioned he was starting a writing group. He knew several people at work who all "kinda, sorta wrote a little," himself included, and he invited me to join.

At our first meeting, Tony told the group a story that—and I know this sounds clichéd, but it's true—changed my life.

He said that when he was in junior high, he was riding the bus home from school and passed a rundown house—no yard, unpainted fence, peeling shutters—and yet, parked in the driveway, polished and perfect and gleaming, was a brand-new white Lamborghini. Tony thought to himself, "Now *there* is a man with priorities. They may not be the *right* priorities, but he has them."

Tony wanted to start a writing group as a way to "buy his Lamborghini." He wanted to make writing a priority in his life. Even if it was hard. Even if it meant sacrificing other things. He wanted to take it seriously. He wanted to get something done.

We were going to stop being "someday" writers; we were going to be "today" writers.

We met every Thursday after work, and we reviewed one another's pages and offered feedback and suggestions. I was good at that part—it was what I did every day in my job.

Then it was my turn to submit some pages to the group. Which meant I had to write something.

I don't remember what I turned in to the group for that first review, but what I do remember is feeling the unparalleled joy of creating something new. Of writing. Of telling a story. Of telling *my* story. It's why I wholeheartedly encourage writers to join a writing group. They are a safe place to fail and a joyous place to succeed.

In addition to your trusted critique group, share your story with people who don't know you. Having a variety of people offer you feedback will result in better feedback.

Remember, however, that once you have gathered all the outside feedback, it's up to you to decide what you want to change and what notes you want to ignore. If several people agree on a problem, it's probably a problem. But if only one person brings up an issue, it might not be that big of a deal.

NOW WHAT?

You've worn your various hats as a writer, a reader, and a self-editor. Check.

You've rotated through your glasses, noting what you love and what might need more work. Check.

You've done some additional analytical work on plot, character, and theme. Check.

So . . . does that mean you're done?

I think the better question is: Are you still building, or are you redecorating?

If the story still has plot holes that need to be patched, thematic framework that needs to be installed, or a new room that needs to be added for a new character, keep building. But if you are fussing with the word choice of blue curtains or green or if you are moving punctuation around like furniture in a room or if you have a minor quibble with the texture of the carpet, then you are probably ready for copyediting.

Chapter 7
A Fistful of Commas

The title of this chapter came from my brother, who said he takes a fistful of commas and throws them at a paragraph and wherever they land is where they stick. Oh, my poor copyediting-loving heart!

And full disclosure, the following rules are gleaned from *The Chicago Manual of Style*, which is the editor's Bible on issues of usage, grammar, punctuation, and style. This chapter is not intended to be a comprehensive or exhaustive discussion. I simply want to share some of the most common questions that come up around copyedits and a few tips on how I remember the rules.

Story Time with Lisa

I once taught a workshop at a writing conference where I gave everyone a writing prompt: a relationship, a setting, a problem, and a favorite word. Then I challenged them to write a thousand words in forty-five minutes using that prompt. After the time was up, I asked the class what surprised them most about the exercise, and the majority said they didn't think they could write that many words in so short a time. They were surprised they could.

Then I asked what was hard about the exercise, and many people said it was hard not to edit while writing.

The instinct to backspace is strong. I personally hate those red squiggly lines under all my misspelled words when I'm drafting, and the urge to go back and fix them is intense. Sometimes, I give in and correct my mistakes, even though I'm trying to keep moving forward.

I also asked the class what was easy about the writing assignment, and many of them said it was easy once they got started—especially when they gave themselves permission to write with abandon.

After everybody had written a thousand words of a hot mess, I walked them through some simple copyediting work to clean up the text.

I think that for many writers, part of their process is to do some "pre-editing" of small errors while writing—just enough to scratch the itch in their creative brain that demands they go back and fix it. Especially if *not* fixing it will keep you from moving forward. For those authors, here is a general round-up of some copyediting rules that, if you can apply them to your manuscript, will help polish it until it shines.

GETTING STARTED

As a general rule, I would encourage you to learn the proof-reading marks. Even though most editing is done electronically these days, it's helpful to know the language of editing and what the symbols mean so you can communicate the changes that you want.

When I'm preparing to copyedit a manuscript, these are some of the quick tasks I do:

- I search for double spaces and replace them with a single space. I don't care if you type two spaces after a period when you're drafting, but do this task before you send the manuscript to anyone else.
- I make sure the document is double-spaced.

Proofreaders' Marks

OPERATIONAL SIGNS

ℒ	Delete
◡	Close up; delete space
ℒ̰	Delete and close up (use only when deleting letters *within* a word)
(stet)	Let it stand
#	Insert space
(eq#)	Make space between words equal; make space between lines equal
(hr#)	Insert hair space
(ls)	Letterspace
¶	Begin new paragraph
□	Indent type one em from left or right
]	Move right
[	Move left
][	Center
⌐	Move up
⌐	Move down
(fl)	Flush left
(fr)	Flush right
=	Straighten type; align horizontally
‖	Align vertically
(tr)	Transpose
(sp)	Spell out

TYPOGRAPHICAL SIGNS

(ital)	Set in italic type
(rom)	Set in roman type
(bf)	Set in boldface type
(lc)	Set in lowercase
(caps)	Set in capital letters
(sc)	Set in small capitals
(wf)	Wrong font; set in correct type
X	Check type image; remove blemish
∨	Insert here *or* make superscript
∧	Insert here *or* make subscript

PUNCTUATION MARKS

∧	Insert comma
∨ ∨	Insert apostrophe *or* single quotation mark
∨ ∨	Insert quotation marks
⊙	Insert period
(set)?	Insert question mark
;/	Insert semicolon
: or :/	Insert colon
=	Insert hyphen
M	Insert em dash
N	Insert en dash
⟨/⟩ or ⟨(|⟩	Insert parentheses

Source: *The Chicago Manual of Style*

- I make sure there are page breaks before each chapter opening and that the chapters are numbered sequentially.
- I make sure the ellipses have spaces between the three dots. (Side note: Ellipses are *always* three dots. If you have a set of four dots, that first dot is a period.)
- I run spell check. Microsoft Word doesn't always catch every error, and I don't always agree with its spelling suggestions, but it's an easy, quick pass to catch the most obvious errors. For everything else, I use Merriam-Webster's 11th Edition Collegiate Dictionary, which you can access online at m-w.com. I always keep the website open on a second monitor, and I look up any word if I have even a hint of a question about its spelling or whether it needs hyphenation. After all, "The most common spelling questions for writers and editors concern compound terms—whether to spell as two words, hyphenate, or close up as a single word. . . . The first place to look for answers is the dictionary."[1]

THE POTENT POWER OF PUNCTUATION!

Punctuation is as critical to your story as your words are. Those tiny marks are the accent markers of emotion, and they tell the reader what and how to feel about your words. Changing a punctuation mark can change the entire meaning and feeling of a sentence. Understanding the basics of each punctuation mark means you'll hold their potent power in the palm of your hand.

Commas

Of the fifteen main punctuation marks—period, question mark, exclamation point, asterisk, en dash, semicolon, brackets, parentheses, ellipsis, em dash, quotation mark, colon, hyphen, apostrophe, and comma—the one that gives most people the most trouble is the comma. That's because commas have the most jobs to do in a sentence and the most rules they need to abide by. This chapter is not going to cover all the rules and regulations that come with commas, but I hope these highlights will help you feel more confident in knowing where the commas go.

Let's start with an easy one. The serial comma, also known as "the Oxford comma," is used in a list of three or more items.

- "A loaf of bread, a container of milk, and a stick of butter."[2]

Another easy rule is that you use commas after introductory words and phrases, such as *Yes* or *No*. However, you don't use commas in the phrases "Oh yeah?" and "Oh no!" when the *Oh* is not an interjection but is part of the phrase. But if you place "oh" before a person's name, you would use a comma: "Oh, Alex."

The comma's usage usually depends on what kind of word it sits next to. Commas and adjectives are great friends, and they like to be close together when they precede a noun. If you can write "adjective and adjective noun," you can also write "adjective, adjective noun." But when adjectives are not coordinate, the comma is booted to the curb.

- The people in line to ride Big Thunder Mountain were noisy, pushy, and impatient.
- For Christmas, she bought an inexpensive blue dress.

Commas are also not invited to parties where the constructions "not . . . but" or "not only . . . but also" are present. However, if these correlative conjunctions are joining two independent clauses, then commas would be used.

- We decided to visit not only Disneyland this year but also Disney World.

Likewise, when the words *too* or *either* are used to mean "also," you can leave the comma at home. However, when *too* is used in the middle of a sentence, a comma can add clarity.

- I like waffles too.
- I, too, decided to order waffles.

Commas and Clauses

Clauses are simply grammatical units of words, and they can be either independent, dependent, or relative. There are other types of clauses, but those three are the most common.

Independent Clauses

An independent clause is a stand-alone sentence with a subject and a verb, and independent clauses love their commas. When independent clauses are joined by the conjunctions *for, and, nor, but, or, yet,* or *so* (FANBOYS), they'll invite the comma along for the ride.

- Sam rarely drove the Impala, but he rode shotgun.

No comma is needed for short clauses that are closely connected.

- Sarah played the harp and David sang.

However, if you have two independent clauses joined by a comma but *without* a conjunction, that is called a comma splice. There are three easy ways to fix it: change the comma to either a semicolon or a period or add a conjunction.

- "Driver picks the music, shotgun shuts his cakehole."[3] (Incorrect, despite the many online memes)
- "Driver picks the music; shotgun shuts his cakehole." (Correct)
- "Driver picks the music. Shotgun shuts his cakehole." (Correct)
- "Driver picks the music, and shotgun shuts his cakehole." (Correct)

Compound Predicates

When deciding whether you need to include a comma in a sentence containing a subject plus multiple verbs, simply count the verbs.

If you have two verbs plus a coordinating conjunction, the sentence is fine without a comma.

- John framed three pictures and sold them to an art collector.

But if you have *more* than two verbs plus a coordinating conjunction, bring on the Oxford comma!

- Nancy drove to the store, stopped by the post office, and gathered some commas to punctuate this sentence.

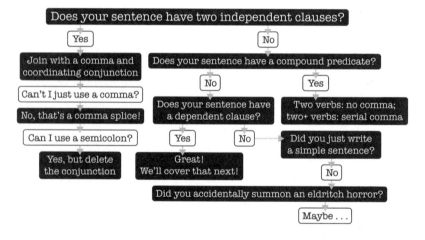

Dependent Clauses

A dependent clause is a phrase that can't stand alone but is linked to an independent clause.

Dependent clauses are tricky because they come in two different types: restrictive and nonrestrictive. I always want "nonrestrictive" to mean "no comma," but it's actually the opposite. (Thanks for nothing, English language!) So the way I try to remember it is that a restrictive dependent clause is restricted to "just you and me," so there's no room for any additional punctuation—not even a comma. That's because a restrictive dependent clause is essential to understanding the independent clause.

- The diver who first discovered Atlantis was hailed as a hero. (We're hailing a specific diver as a hero, not just any diver.)

A nonrestrictive dependent clause, however, is *not* essential to fully understanding the main clause, which means it can come and go as it pleases, and it can bring all the punctuation to the party it wants—including all the commas.

- Walter, the diver who graduated from college last year, teaches classes at the local YMCA. (The extra information about Walter's college graduation can be deleted without changing the meaning of the sentence.)

When an introductory dependent clause precedes the independent clause, it needs a comma. Think of the comma as a name tag, and it's polite to introduce the clause with it.

- Until I have checked the commas, I cannot approve this sentence.

But when a restrictive dependent clause *follows* an independent clause, you don't need to use a comma.

- Brittany celebrated when she heard the news about Walter's new job.

Relative Clauses

A relative clause is a dependent clause introduced by a relative pronoun. Relative pronouns include *whose, whoever, whomever, who,* and *whom,* but we are going to focus on the two most common relative pronouns: *which* and *that.*

Which is used nonrestrictively to add information about an item already identified. Nonrestrictive relative clauses introduced by *which* need commas. (Because nonrestrictive clauses are not opposed to having a comma join the party.)

- The sculpture, which was made of marble, was submitted to the contest on time.

That is used restrictively to narrow a category or identify a particular item being talked about. Restrictive relative clauses introduced by *that* don't need commas. (Because restrictive clauses don't want any punctuation to come between them.)

- The sculpture that the artist submitted to the contest was made of marble.

An easy rule of thumb that helps me remember the difference is that "which"s have tails (commas) and "that"s don't. I imagine a witch on a broomstick, which looks like a tail, and a bat, which does not have a tail, to help me use this principle correctly.

Appositives

An appositive is a word, name, phrase, or clause placed next to a noun to provide an explanatory equivalent. Appositives can be restrictive or nonrestrictive, and by following the rules we have discussed, it's easy to figure out where the commas go by determining what information is essential to the noun.

- John and his son, Adam, went to a baseball game together. (The commas around the name *Adam* indicate that John only has one son. That information is not essential to the noun, thus it is nonrestrictive, and it calls for commas.)
- John's son Sam studied to be a lawyer. (Because there are no commas around the name *Sam*, it means that John has more than one son. That information *is* essential to the noun; thus, it is restrictive, and it does not need commas.)

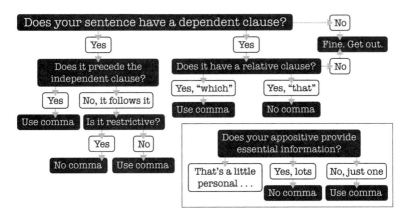

Commas and Phrases

Commas also are used in descriptive, participial, and adverbial phrases. As with clauses, there are other types of phrases, but those three are the most common. And as with clauses, descriptive phrases can also be restrictive or nonrestrictive, which means they follow the same rules: a restrictive phrase has no need for a comma, while a nonrestrictive phrase does.

- The cat with the stuffed bird in his paws is named Loki.
- Loki, with a stuffed bird in his paws, meowed and rolled onto his back.

Commas can move around in a participial phrase, either appearing after the introductory phrase or when the phrase appears in the middle (unless it's restrictive) or at the end (unless it's restrictive).

- Having forgotten his passport, Rufus was forced to stand aside.
- Rufus, having forgotten his passport, was forced to stand aside.
- Rufus was forced to stand aside, having forgotten his passport.

Commas can also be used after the introductory adverbial phrase or when the adverbial phrase is in the middle of a sentence.

- With three consecutive pitches, Henry struck out the final batter to win the game.
- Henry, with three consecutive pitches, struck out the final batter to win the game.

Apostrophes

Adding an apostrophe to a word makes it possessive, not plural. If you need to make a noun plural, add an *s*. (Unless the noun ends in *ch*, *j*, *s*, *sh*, *x*, or *z*—then add *es* to make it plural.)

- Bilbo's ring
- Shakespeare's pen
- Moses's staff

Adding an apostrophe to a plural noun also makes it possessive.

- puppies' paws (lots of puppies have lots of paws)
- the Lincolns' house (more than one Lincoln lives at the house)

Semicolons

If you have two independent clauses *not* joined by a conjunction, you can use a semicolon to signal a closer connection than a period would create.

- Though she's driven all over the Midwest, Shauna has never been to the beach; she hopes to visit there one day.

You can also use a semicolon with the conjunctive adverbs *however*, *thus*, *hence*, *indeed*, *accordingly*, *besides*, and *therefore*.

- The opera singer came down with a cold; therefore, the Saturday matinee was canceled.

When items in a series contain internal punctuation, use a semicolon for clarity.

- The number of raffle tickets purchased was as follows: Ruth, 4; Kim, 5; Bri, 1; Jody, 3; Donna, 7.

I once attended a punctuation class at an editing conference, and an attendee mentioned how her boss had gone rogue with this rule, and the entire room nearly rioted. After class, I tweeted: "You haven't lived until you're in a room with 50 editors, all bristling at the idea of not using a semicolon to subdivide lists within a main list."

Colons

The colon's main function is to introduce a list, but not every list.

- Santa usually wears three layers: an undershirt, a vest, and a red jacket.
- The car's trunk held a spare tire, a blanket, and a first aid kit.

Do you capitalize the word after a colon? Yes, if it's a proper noun or if the text that follows the colon is a grammatically complete sentence.

- Elizabeth had to make a choice: She could take a vacation to Italy. She could attend her parents' fiftieth wedding anniversary. Or she could host her high school reunion.

Dashes

The *dash* comes in three lengths: the shortest is a hyphen, the middle is an en dash, and the longest is an em dash.

An easy rule of thumb for me is that hyphens are used between words, en dashes are used between numbers, and em dashes are used between thoughts. The bigger the item, the longer the dash.

Hyphens are important because these things are not the same:

- Twenty four-hour shifts (20 shifts lasting four hours each)
- Twenty-four hour shifts (24 shifts lasting one hour each)
- Twenty-four-hour shifts (an indeterminate number of shifts lasting 24 hours each)

Determining whether a word is hyphenated is a question best answered by the dictionary. I look up words all the time to see if they are open, closed, or hyphenated. *Chicago* has a lengthy chart of rules for hyphenated words. With a subscription, you can download a PDF of the chart from *The Chicago Manual of Style* website. I have my PDF saved on my computer desktop for easy access.

One quick note about hyphens: If you're using an *-ly* adverb plus an adjective or a participle, the phrase is not hyphenated.

- Mary was exceptionally intelligent.
- Michael was smartly dressed.
- Emily sat in the dimly lit study, reading a book of magical spells.

Hyphens are also essential for clarity. There is a difference, after all, between "re-creation" and "recreation." And you can suspend hyphenation if you have a series of constructions.

- The bag was filled with five-, ten-, and twenty-dollar bills.

Finally, you use hyphens to separate letters when spelling out a w-o-r-d in dialogue.

En dashes are mostly used to separate ranges of dates, times, and page numbers.

Em dashes are used to set off an explanatory element—or to denote an abrupt break in thought.

- The Singer family—Bobby, Ellen, and Jo—enjoyed their trip to South Dakota.

When punctuating dialogue, an em dash denotes an interruption, while ellipses denote a character trailing off in thought. You can also use em dashes when adding an action beat that interrupts the dialogue.

- "The murderer is—" A conk on the head prevented her from finishing her accusation.
- "I don't know . . ." he trailed off, lost in thought.
- "Don't you dare"—his voice broke—"think that there is anything, past or present, that I would put in front of you!"[4]

Parentheses

Parentheses require the buddy system. They come in pairs and travel in pairs and stay in pairs. They are used to set off material (like this) from the surrounding text. Parentheses are rarely used in fiction unless as an aside to the reader, and even then, I would probably recommend against it. Em dashes might be the better choice.

Quotation Marks

Quotation marks are most often used in dialogue, and they also require the buddy system. If you have a set of opening quotation marks, you'll need a set of closing quotation marks too. The only exception is when your quoted material or character dialogue continues through multiple paragraphs; then you have opening quotation marks at the beginning of each paragraph and closing quotation marks at the end of the last paragraph.

When a word is being used as itself, it's either italicized or enclosed in quotation marks.

- She clicked *Buy* on the website, completing her Christmas shopping.

Quotation marks are not used for emphasis. Instead, those are called "scare quotes," and they identify nonstandard or ironic usage. Overuse of them can irritate readers—or make them laugh.

- "Fresh" donuts
- Professional "massage"

Titles of Things

When it comes to punctuating titles of things, they will either be italicized, set in roman type, or enclosed in quotation marks, depending on what the item is.

- Italics: book titles, movies, journals, blogs, video games, TV shows, plays, podcasts, paintings, ships, and newspapers.

- Roman: book series, websites, board games, TV or streaming networks, buildings, and monuments.
- Quotation marks: poems; songs; TV episode titles; titles of articles found in magazines, newspapers, or blogs; fairy tales; and nursery rhymes.

The way I remember which is which is that if it's a big story, like a book or movie or TV show, that's a heavy story, so it has to sit on a shelf—which, in proofreading terms, is an underline, which signals that those words need to be italicized.

Poems, songs, an individual episode title, or a magazine article are little and small and can be hung on hooks (quotation marks).

WORDS TO WATCH

In addition to paying attention to the fiddly little punctuation marks, keep an eye out for small words and phrases during the copyediting stage that I think deserve a second look.

Phrases to check: *a bit, a little, a little bit, a lot,* and *at some point.*

These phrases may have crept into your manuscript during the drafting stage, and the truth is, you may not need many of them. You'll want to check each one and evaluate its usefulness, but I'll bet nine times out of ten, those filler phrases can be deleted without issue.

Verbs

We talked in chapter three about active and passive voice and the importance of keeping an eye on those "to be" verbs: *am, are, been, being, is, was,* and *were.* If you haven't already done so, take some time to search your manuscript for each of these words to see if they are still the best option for the sentence. If not, maybe it's time to exchange them for a stronger, more specific verb.

You can also upgrade other verbs that could benefit from a more evocative word.

For example:

- not *sat* but *crouched*
- not *ran* but *scampered*
- not *went* but *crawled*
- not *looked* but *spied*
- not *got* but *captured*

Other verbs to watch for could include *appears, appeared to, begin to* or *beginning to, can, decide, feel* or *felt like, got, heard, look, realize, see, saw, seems* or *seemed to, shrugged, start, thought,* and *watch.*

Again, these verbs may be doing the best job in the manuscript, in which case they can stay. You may not need to eliminate every single instance of every single one of these verbs. The exercise is to find them, evaluate them, and ask yourself: Would a more specific verb be stronger here? Could it help streamline the prose?

Avoid Redundancy

While you are looking at your verbs, keep an eye out for ways to avoid redundancy. For example, "nodded her head" could simply be "nodded" because what other body part can you nod? (In American Sign Language, of course, you can move your fist up and down to communicate nodding, but other than that . . .)

"Sat down" could simply be "sat" because the "down" is implied. The same logic applies to "stood" and "knelt."

Adjectives

Adjectives add personality and flair to your manuscript, but too many of them can be overwhelming, so make sure your adjectives are specifically descriptive. Some adjectives to watch for and perhaps eliminate from your manuscript include *awesome, definite, fantastic,* and *super.* These words can either be adjectives or adverbs and warrant a closer look: *almost, great, just, like,* and *very.*

When it comes to adjective analysis, here are three quick tips to keep in mind:

- Not every noun needs an adjective.
- Don't stack too many adjectives in a row. (You're not playing Jenga here.)
- Avoid repetition. A "violet-colored ribbon" can simply be a "violet ribbon" because "violet" is already identified as a color.

Adverbs

People have strong feelings about adverbs. Some authors say you should never use them. I take the approach that adverbs are an official part of speech. They have a job to do—namely, to describe or modify a verb, adjective, or another adverb—and if they are doing that job better than any other word could, then they can stay. You have my permission to use an adverb if you need to.

That said, you'll want to make sure you're not overusing adverbs. There's a long list of *-ly* words that are worth watching for and perhaps eliminating from your manuscript: *absolutely, actually, basically, certainly, definitely, essentially, honestly, hopefully, literally, nearly, obviously, particularly, positively, probably, really, seriously, slightly, totally, truly, virtually.*

There are even some non-*ly* adverbs to keep an eye on: *anyway, nevertheless, often, quite, rather,* and *somehow.*

Adverbs seem to show up frequently in dialogue tags, and I think it's acceptable to use them as much as you like while drafting your manuscript. But when you're doing an editorial pass, try to change those adverbs to a more specific verb. For example, "said loudly" could simply be "shouted" and "said quietly" could be "whispered."

The goal of all this searching and evaluating and fussing with commas and hyphens and individual words is to make sure your story—and your prose—is watertight. Focused, specific language is powerful and memorable. You want to give your reader the opportunity to move beyond the words on the page and sink wholeheartedly into the story.

Story Time with Lisa

Brandon Mull is a #1 *New York Times* best-selling author many times over. He has published dozens and dozens of books, but he got his start at Shadow Mountain with *Fablehaven*. That was the start of a five-book series that grew into ten books with the addition of the Dragonwatch series. He also wrote three books in the Candy Shop War series.

I was not Brandon's editor for all of those books, but when his editor at Shadow Mountain retired and Brandon turned in the last book of the Candy Shop War—*Carnival Quest*—it fell to me to step up to the plate.

I will admit I felt intimidated. I knew the manuscript had gone through Brandon's personal group of beta readers plus a detailed developmental edit with my boss, Chris Schoebinger, before it landed on my desk. I also knew Brandon had worked with several editors at big national publishing houses and had received much-deserved acclaim for his writing, and I didn't want to let him down.

I poured myself into the edit to help Brandon make the book the best it could be, and I did what I do for every book: I tightened the prose, I checked the grammar and the spelling and the punctuation. I queried possible plot holes. I made suggestions. I gave him my emotional reactions. I praised the language I loved, questioned the story points I thought could be strengthened. I asked for feedback from several sensitivity readers.

Then I got to this paragraph:

"The Swindler's attraction looked exactly like the building at the physical carnival. The glittering sign was in the same font, and the building was the same size."

I tightened the prose until it read like this:

"The Swindler's shop looked exactly like the building in the physical carnival down to the font on the glittering sign."[5]

Brandon left a comment for me in the file: "This is one of SO MANY examples where you streamline text and improve fluidity with great excellence. Any such streamlining I don't tamper with was streamlining I admired."

What was even better was that Brandon told the same thing to my boss: "Lisa has a real talent for streamlining language sometimes. Making it smoother and more elegant."

I didn't realize I had developed a skill in streamlining prose until an author with such experience pointed it out to me. (Just between you and me, I mentally edit his comment to delete the word *sometimes*.)

YOU DON'T HAVE TO BE AN EXPERT

If this all feels like a lot, don't worry. You don't have to be an expert in either developmental editing or copyediting. (That's my job.) If you find that you are better at developmental editing than copyediting, don't worry. You can always find someone who is strong in the areas where you might feel weak. Remember, you don't have to learn all the ins and outs of grammar, spelling, and punctuation all at once. Implement a few rules at a time until the process becomes instinctive.

I sometimes joke with my authors that I can cut 5,000 words out of their manuscript and they'd never even notice. (I have, and they haven't.)

Could you cut 5,000 words from *your* manuscript? I bet you can!

GET PUBLISHED

Chapter 8
Submissions and the Slush Pile

You've written your book. You've done your developmental editing and some light copyediting. Now it's time to send your story out into the world for people to read.

Don't panic! Yes, it can be scary putting your work on display. What if no one likes it?

Oh, but what if they do?

And what if the very thing you wrote becomes the very thing someone else needs to hear?

Story Time with Lisa

It was a new office; no one had worked there yet. The building was new, the position was new. I was new. It was my first day as an editorial assistant at Bookcraft, and I was excited and terrified.

I had a desk, a chair, an electric typewriter, and a box filled with four months' worth of manuscripts that had been read and rejected, but no one had told the authors yet. Stacked on the bookcase next to the box were even more manuscripts that nobody had even looked at.

That was my introduction to the slush pile. I'd been hired to take care of it.

I immediately made a chart of the manuscripts that had come in, the manuscripts that were going out, and who needed to read what. I felt like I had been thrown into the deep end of the pool, and I was frantically trying to figure out how to swim. But I quickly learned that there was no place I'd rather be than swimming in brand-new stories from hopeful authors.

Before we dive too deeply into the slush pile, I want to mention that your manuscript may end up swimming in several slush piles before reaching a bookstore shelf. That's because there is an important person who is part of the chain of submissions, reviews, and acceptances: the literary agent.

LITERARY AGENTS

There may still be some small to midsized publishers who allow unsolicited manuscripts, but by and large, if you want an editor at a publishing house to read your manuscript, you'll need an agent to make sure it gets there.

The process generally looks like this: you submit your manuscript to an agent's slush pile. The agent will read your query letter and manuscript and decide whether they are willing to represent you to a publisher. If so, the agent will submit your manuscript to an editor's slush pile. The editor will read that submission and decide whether they are willing to publish your book.

Finding an agent is like online dating. You want to find someone who likes the same things you like, who you think you might be able to get along with, and then you knock on their proverbial email door with your manuscript in hand and ask, "Do you like this?" and you hope they say yes.

The advice and suggestions I'll share in this section apply equally to agents and editors because both agents and editors deal with submissions, query letters, and pitching. I can recommend the websites AgentQuery.com and QueryTracker.net as excellent places to start your search for an agent.

I WANT TO SAY YES

As somebody who reads manuscripts—both unsolicited manuscripts and those submitted by an agent—I can honestly say that I am looking for reasons to say yes to your submission. I want to find the right story for our company to publish, the *best* story to publish. We want your book to succeed.

When I find a mistake in your query letter or your manuscript—because there *will* be a mistake—the first question I ask is, "Is this fixable?" A typo is an easy fix. A missing word is an easy fix. A misplaced comma or two (or more) is an easy fix.

Other mistakes might be more problematic. Are there point-of-view shifts? Is the pacing uneven? Are the characters unlikable? Is the plot too complicated to follow? Did I fall down a plot hole?

Are those mistakes fixable? Yes, they are.

Should I be the one to fix them? No. That's your job.

The more mistakes you can find and fix prior to submission, the better chance your manuscript will have of being accepted.

It's also important to remember this key truth: Writing is a personal expression. Book buying is often an emotional choice. But publishing is a business. We want to buy your book from you then sell it to other people, so everyone makes money.

FOUR THINGS YOU CAN'T CONTROL

When it comes to publishing and submissions in the slush pile, however, there are some things you simply can't control.

1. The number of manuscripts submitted to a publisher in a given year.
2. The number of available slots a publisher has for new writers.

3. Other submitted manuscripts that might be similar to yours.

4. My time, emotions, or other responsibilities.

So Many Authors

Spoiler Alert: There are other people besides you writing a book right now. You can't control that. Nor can you control whether they finish or who they're going to submit to. They might be hoping to submit to the same publisher you have your eye on, and they might even be polishing a manuscript that is in the same genre as yours. The best thing you can do is focus on your own project and not worry about what anyone else is doing.

Only So Many Spots

Because publishing is a business, and because we want to make money, we make financial decisions based on how many books we can reasonably afford to publish in a given year, how many books we think we will sell, and how much money we think we will make.

We have a set number of slots on our publishing schedule, and we want books that will fill a variety of genres as well as target multiple age groups. When building a schedule for a new year, I begin by dropping in the projects from our previously published authors who are either writing an ongoing series or have written another stand-alone story. These are authors who have proven themselves in the marketplace and who have readers eagerly awaiting their next book.

Then, as an editorial team, we identify the "holes" in the list. What kinds of books should we have but don't? Some of those spots will be filled by authors who we approach and ask to write a specific book for us.

In the end, there may be only one or two available spots for a debut author. I know, the math is daunting. We review hundreds and hundreds of manuscripts every year, and we pick one, maybe two, of those? But I take great pride in the fact that we've always found room for a brand-new, first-time, never-before-been-published debut author somewhere on the Shadow Mountain list.

Not only *can* it happen, but it also *does* happen. Maybe this year, it will happen to you. But you can't control whether there is a spot waiting for you to fill.

Only So Many Stories

Every so often, I'll start to see patterns emerge in the slush pile—similar stories submitted at the same time. It could be because people have picked up on a popular trend in the marketplace and are writing a similar kind of story. Back when *Twilight* was popular, I had four young adult novel submissions about vampires in one month.

The danger of writing to a trend, however, is that usually by the time a trend is identified, it's already starting to wane. There are always exceptions, but trends are designed to come and go, and publishing is a long process. If we accept a manuscript that fits a hot trend, we have to hope it will still be popular in two years.

It's a delicate balance, trying to ride an existing wave versus being the first of whatever is coming next. If the book you've written doesn't have many current comps in the marketplace, perhaps you've written about a topic that people aren't interested in at the moment. Or it could be that you've identified a hole in the marketplace, and your story will fill it and create a brand-new trend. It's hard to know which side you fall on, and it's hard for publishers to predict which of all the similar manuscripts on our table will be the one that breaks through.

So Many Busy Days

Manuscript acquisition agents and editors are human too. We have bad days. We get grumpy. We get tired. And we can sometimes get angry at how many manuscripts we have to read.

Get Published.

Reading submissions usually falls last on my to-do list, not because it's a task I don't like but because I have more urgent deadlines for other projects. My days are stuffed with meetings and other tasks that make it difficult to pay attention to the slush pile.

Which is why, at the beginning of my career, I decided to set aside Friday mornings to read manuscripts. I am usually finished with the bulk of my weekly work by Friday, and I am looking forward to the weekend, which means traditionally, I am in a pretty good mood.

I feel that the manuscript I am about to look at in the slush pile deserves me at my best. The author poured their heart and soul and blood and sweat and tears into their manuscript, and they were brave enough to send it to me to see if I would like it—maybe even publish it. It isn't fair to them if I come to that manuscript grumpy or in a bad mood, so whenever I start to feel tired, or if I'm hungry and need lunch, I'll stop looking at manuscripts because I don't want to say no to a manuscript that maybe deserved a yes just because I was tired.

That said, perhaps not all editors or agents have the luxury of setting aside a manuscript until they are in a better mood. You don't know exactly when your manuscript will be reviewed or the circumstances surrounding that review. You'll just have to trust the process.

FOUR THINGS YOU CAN CONTROL

Now that we have the bad news out of the way, let's get to the good news. There are some things you *can* control when it comes to the submission process.

1. Do your homework.
2. Follow submission guidelines.
3. Write a compelling cover letter. (We'll talk about how to do this in chapter nine.)
4. Deal with rejection.

160

Do Your Homework

We talked about the importance of wearing different hats during the editing and revision process, but at some point, you'll want to take off your writer hat and put on your business hat and start to think like a publisher. Here are six questions I encourage every author to answer before submitting a manuscript:

Question #1: Am I in the right slush pile? It seems like this should go without saying, but don't send your young adult fantasy to a fly-fishing magazine. That may sound extreme, and perhaps it is, but we still get poetry submissions despite our guidelines clearly saying we don't accept poetry. You want to give your manuscript the best shot for success, which means you want to be in the right place for an editor to find you.

Question #2: Who's going to buy this? You need to find and know your audience. Will your book be purchased mostly by teachers and librarians? Will your book be purchased as a gift? Are you aiming for readers of a specific genre or story trope?

Are you writing for nine- to twelve-year-olds? Are you writing for sixteen-year-olds? Are you writing for adults, ages twenty to forty? I sometimes receive query letters promising that the accompanying manuscript is "perfect for ages eight to eighty," and I shake my head because those two age groups read very different kinds of books. The more specific you can be about your audience helps a publisher know who to market your book to.

Question #3: How is my book different? Be clear about what is special about your book. What is it that will make it rise to the top of the charts? What makes your book marketable? What is the one thing you could say about your book in order to convince someone to buy it? The answer to this question should be clearly communicated in your pitch.

Dig deep into the uniqueness of your story. I've seen query letters offering up "well-developed characters and a compelling plot" as unique features. That is the bare minimum I expect from a submission. What was the spark of the idea that made you keep writing? Tell me that.

Question #4: What are people buying? This question is about trends and topics. While you, as an author, will not have access to hard sales data from publishers, you can still look at top ten lists at the bookstore, keep abreast of *The New York Times* or the *USA Today* bestseller lists, and watch Amazon rankings or review Goodreads lists to see if there are patterns emerging. Read the *Publishers Weekly* deal report or browse Manuscript Wish List or Writer's Digest to see what agents are buying.

A lot of agents, editors, and publishers are also on social media, and following them can give you a great insight into their personality, what they're publishing, and what they're looking for.

Those may sound pretty basic, but they are, in fact, the exact same resources publishers, agents, and editors are looking at to see what people are buying.

Question #5: What is my marketing plan? The publishing industry has changed since I started my career, and one of the major components of success I've seen shift is the need for the author's involvement in marketing and selling the book. Authors continue to be highly involved in the process, and that's good for everyone. It does require that you wear your business hat, however, and look at your manuscript not as a work of art but as a product and brainstorm ways of how you are going to sell it. Creativity is your commodity—you are selling your imagination and your ability to create.

Those marketing plans may go beyond book signings or school visits, newsletters, or social media postings. Attending writing conferences or teaching can be a great way to introduce yourself to new readers, as are doing library visits and interviews for websites, podcasts, radio, or television. If you show up with something to say, people will pay attention.

You may need to think outside the box in order to make suggestions for your publisher to consider.

Story Time with Lisa

My book *After Hello* is a contemporary young adult love story, and part of the storyline involves trading something small for something bigger and then trading it again for something else until you get what you really want. In the book, the characters do this kind of trading, starting with a sugar packet, the kind that restaurants leave on the table for your coffee.

For the release of the book, I asked my publisher if we could print the book title and the company's logo on some sugar packets that I could then give away to people as part of a tie-in for the story. It was a fun promotional item, and it gave me lots of opportunities to talk to people about the book.

Question #6: Have I asked five people to give me honest feedback? Sometimes the most honest reviews come from people who don't know you personally. You'll also want those readers to be part of your target audience. A critical move is joining a writing group or finding critique partners who will read your book and give you feedback about the plot structure, character arcs, and thematic development of your story. They can help you troubleshoot any problems before you submit your manuscript.

Finding a writing group could be as simple as asking a couple of friends to join you on your journey. Or you may be able to connect with other authors via social media or at in-person events, such as writing conferences. When forming (or joining) a writing group, it can be wise to gather with other authors who write either in the same genre as you or for the same audience as you. But there is also value in joining a group with writers across the spectrum of genres and audiences, as they will bring different perspectives to the table.

Follow Submission Guidelines

Most literary agents have their submission guidelines posted online, available for review. Find them, read them, love them, live by them.

Submission requirements are fairly standard in the industry, but the devil is in the details, as they say, and you'll want to be familiar with each agent's specific requirements. In general, you'll need to provide a cover letter that includes your contact information, a synopsis of the story, the title, the genre, the word count, and a short biography. Agents may ask for five pages, a limited number of chapters, or the entire manuscript.

When it comes to your contact information, please include a link to your web page or social media accounts. I don't always look up authors online, but if I'm really interested in a manuscript or in you, I will check out your website to see what kind of content you have or if you have a longer biography that can help me get to know you better. I might look you up on social media to see what kind of influence you have or what your reach is. Social media numbers can be valuable for marketing purposes, but they rarely are deal breakers—or deal makers—when it comes to accepting a manuscript. I'm most interested in seeing activity, engagement, and enthusiasm. When I'm stalking an author on social media, I like to see authors who are being themselves. Yes, it's okay to encourage people to buy your book once in a while, but if every single post is simply "buy my book," that type of content is less engaging, and people—including me—will click away.

Some submission guidelines will also specify what you can expect in terms of a reply. Sometimes, no answer means a no. Some agents or editors will reply to every submission, though that response could take six weeks—or sixteen.

While a manuscript is under review, you may be curious about where your manuscript is, especially if a publisher has had it for a while. Again, the submission guidelines will be your friend because they might contain information about the protocol for asking for a status update. If the guidelines don't mention that detail, I would encourage you to wait the required number of weeks, as posted in the guidelines, before emailing the agent or editor. Even then, I would suggest keeping the email short: "It's been X weeks. Just checking to see if you still have my manuscript under review."

I mention that only because sometimes I will get such an email, and I'll go to check on the submission, and it will turn out that I never received the manuscript in the first place. (Thankfully, that doesn't happen often.)

Fair warning—you'll want to email for a status update only once because it's really easy to say no to someone who emails two or three or four times to ask about a manuscript. I've had people submit a manuscript on Monday and email me on Friday to see if I've made a decision about their book yet. (No. No, I have not.)

Submit your manuscript, and then move on to your next project.

Word Counts

Not all submission guidelines include word counts, but it's good to be aware of the ballpark figures. Often when people ask me about word counts, I jokingly say, "Use as many words as it takes to tell the story. No more and no less."

Word counts can vary from publisher to publisher, but in general, here are my suggestions for where you should be aiming:

- General Fiction: 70K to 90K
- Romance: 60K to 80K
- Sci-fi or Fantasy: 90K to 100K
- Historical: 90K to 100K

- YA Fiction: 50K to 70K
- Middle-Grade Fiction (ages eight to twelve): 30K to 50K
- Picture Books: 500 to 600 words

Word counts matter to publishers because longer books are more expensive to produce. If you can tell a compelling and complete story in sixty thousand words, you might have an edge over a manuscript that is pushing eighty thousand words.

Deal with Rejection

I once estimated that I had sent more than 35,000 rejection letters over the years, which, as my friend Jen pointed out, amounts to the population of a small city.

I'm sorry to say that most rejection letters are form letters, and that is simply because I don't have time to send personalized and detailed letters to every author who submits a manuscript with advice on what to fix and how to fix it. If I receive ten submissions a week, and if it takes me fifteen minutes to write a letter, that's two and a half hours a week spent working on manuscripts that we are *not* going to publish. Over the course of a month, that adds up to ten hours—more than a whole days' worth of work—and I need to spend that time on the books we have accepted for publication.

However, if a manuscript shows promise and if the decision was really close, I might send a "revise and resubmit" letter. I don't mind writing those letters.

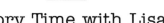

Story Time with Lisa

An agent submitted a manuscript by Laura Ojeda Melchor, and it was a middle-grade contemporary novel about two sisters dealing with grief and sorrow and strength. I loved the emotional writing, the poignant voice, and the compelling story.

But I also felt like it needed some work.

I emailed the agent with a "revise and resubmit" request and said, "I think the protagonist sounds older than a twelve-year-old. I think there's some repetition in her motivation that has started to feel clunky, and I feel like the ending needs to be adjusted."

About a year later, the manuscript came back to me. The author had fixed the voice, taken a good, long look at the pacing, and fixed the plot holes I had mentioned. I was so impressed with her revisions and how she had strengthened the story that I recommended it for publication, and it was accepted. It was released as *Missing Oaklee*, and it is a beautiful, quiet story with lush description and a touching message of hope.

But not every manuscript is either a rejection or a "revise and resubmit." Some submissions take a different path.

Story Time with Lisa

The manuscript had everything I was looking for. It had a spunky main character. It was a middle-grade novel in verse with exquisite writing. It was all about faith and family, and it came from a Black, Indigenous, (and) People of Color (BIPOC) author. The early reviews from our readers were giving it thumbs-ups and gold stars.

I read the book in one sitting on a Saturday afternoon, and I loved it so much I read it again the next day. It checked all the boxes and then some for me, and I was so enthusiastic about the project, I couldn't wait to have it pitched in our editorial meeting. I couldn't wait for the team to say yes.

They said no.

Dear Reader, when I tell you that I wept when I heard the news, I am not exaggerating.

That was the hardest rejection letter I've ever had to write.

———————

It's Not You, It's Me

Sometimes, a rejection letter is sent because the writing or the story isn't as strong or as marketable as we would like. But sometimes, it's not you, it's us. You might get a rejection simply because the market has changed. It might be that we already have a project like yours on the schedule, or it might be that the external cost of business is just too high. As a business, we have to care deeply about how much paper costs and how the supply chain is flowing, all the way down to the price of gas.

Throughout the submission process, I hope you learn to give yourself grace.

There are so many moving pieces in the publishing world, so many voices, so many votes. In many ways, we're all guessing.

I know that slogging your way through the query trenches can be disheartening. Rejection letters can fall like bombs from above, and you're just trying to make your way through the battlefield and the shrapnel, hoping to get to stable ground.

But success is possible. It *does* happen. In my heart, I still hold firm to the belief that good books get published.

Remember the manuscript I loved and lost? About a year after I sent a rejection letter, the author posted on Instagram that the book had found a home at another publishing house. I literally cheered!

I know many authors who have gone the self-publishing route and been successful both financially and creatively. Just because your book hasn't yet been published doesn't automatically mean that it's a bad book or that you're a bad author. It might just mean that you haven't found the right place yet for your story or the right path that will lead you there.

I hope you know that wherever you are on your writing journey, it's important to celebrate your uniqueness. You are telling a story that has never been told before because no one has told it quite the way you have. A rejection of a manuscript is not a rejection of you as a person. It doesn't change your worth. It doesn't change your value.

SLUSH PILE SUCCESS STORIES

Laura Ojeda Melchor's story is just one example of a "slush pile success." And even after all these years of being an editor, I still love finding a diamond in the rough. I've plucked a number of authors out of the slush pile during my career, and some of them have gone on to publish several books with us, others have made the leap to publishing houses in New York, and some are authors who are at the beginning of their journey.

Ally Condie

Ally is at the top of my list because she was the first author I worked with every step of the way, from being a "slush pile find" all the way through sending her book to press.

She sent in three chapters of a young adult novel called *Yearbook*, and each chapter was written by a different character at a high school for each month of the year. I read the pages, and I remember chapter three ended on a kiss, and I was so impressed with her writing that I wrote her back and said, "Please send me the whole manuscript."

She did, and I read it. I liked it even more.

I wrote her back and said, "I don't think you should have twelve points of view. I think you should have four." Some of the characters interacted with each other, but not all of them did, and I found I wasn't as engaged with the individual characters because I knew I was going to read about them only in one chapter. But if I knew that the story would come back to those characters, I suspected I would feel a stronger pull.

She reworked the book and sent it back.

I read it again, and I said, "That's great. But I don't think you picked the right four points of view. Try again?"

Another revision. Another read through. And this time I knew in my bones it was exactly what we were looking for.

I got to tell Ally that we were going to officially accept her book for publication and that I would be her editor. It was the first time a book I'd found, that I'd championed, was going to get published.

Ally told me later that out of everybody she sent those first three chapters to, I was the only person who asked to see the full manuscript. Lucky me.

I worked with Ally for her next four books, and not only did she get better as a writer with each book, but I also got better as an editor, and we became good friends.

Jason F. Wright

The James Miracle was a short adult contemporary novel by Jason F. Wright, and I mostly remember it because the author sent along a little wooden sailboat that he wanted to have packaged with the book because it played an important role in the story. In the end, we rejected the manuscript.

A while later, Jason sent in another short adult contemporary novel, this time Christmas-related, called *Christmas Jars and Hope*, and I read the entire manuscript during lunch one day. The heart of the book was a tradition of collecting spare change in a jar throughout the year and then giving it away anonymously at Christmastime. I finished the manuscript and thought, "We'll call it *Christmas Jars*, sell it with a jar, and it'll be a thing. This could totally work."

I gave the manuscript to Chris and eagerly awaited his review. He, too, read the book in one sitting and then said, "I feel strongly we can sell 20,000 units of this book." The manuscript traveled through the various review and approval processes, and we published the book in 2005. It ended up on the *New York Times* bestseller list and has inspired a hardback edition, two more companion novels, a children's picture book, a collector's edition, a cookbook, and a movie.

Josi S. Kilpack

Josi is an amazing writer, prolific and delightful in every way. She'd already written five books before I got a hold of her manuscript *Unsung Lullaby*. The story dealt with the issue of infertility, and the opening scene of the female protagonist attending a baby shower when she herself was unable to have children was exactly how I felt, having personally experienced the same thing.

I recommended the book for publication, it was accepted, and it became the first in a long list of titles that I got to work on with Josi. After a couple more books, I asked Josi what she was working on next, and she said she had a culinary mystery in mind. That book became *Lemon Tart* and was the first of thirteen mysteries we published.

When Josi mentioned she was ready to move out of mystery, we welcomed her into our Proper Romance line, where she wrote thirteen romances for us, earning four starred reviews and a *Publishers Weekly* Best Romance Book of the Year honor.

She's continued to publish books with other houses as well as with Shadow Mountain, and she has developed a large and passionate following. But it all started with the first chapter of *Unsung Lullaby* that spoke to my heart.

Amy Willoughby-Burle

Not all of our submissions come to us through an agent, but Amy's did. I was hooked by the first paragraph. By the end of five pages, I emailed the agent and said, "I love this. I can't wait to finish reading it. I am extremely interested in this project."

We hadn't done a lot of contemporary women's fiction, but this manuscript was such a sweet, poignant, and heartfelt story of family and a generational exploration of love and trust, and I loved every word of it. We published it as *The Lemonade Year*, and Amy became a dear, close friend of mine.

I mention this particular story because so far, *The Lemonade Year* is the only book Shadow Mountain has published with Amy. Not for lack of trying. She sent in another manuscript, but it didn't quite match what we were looking for. We suggested some ideas for her to try and worked with her on revisions, but nothing quite clicked. She ultimately published those other manuscripts elsewhere, and I hope I can work with Amy again someday.

I share this story as a reminder that every individual "yes" is a singular occurrence, and while we hope that every acceptance can grow into a long-term relationship with multiple books that we can publish together, that isn't always the case. It doesn't mean Amy is a bad writer. It doesn't mean we're a bad publisher. It's about finding the right book with the right publisher at the right time.

Tyler Whitesides

When I first met Tyler Whitesides, I think I might've scared him to death.

I was spending the afternoon at a publisher's fair at a local college, talking to students and answering questions. I had about five or six students at my table when a young man walked up. I invited him to join the conversation, and he said he was actually hoping he could pitch to me. He had driven more than two hours to this event in the hopes he could talk to me.

I looked at the group of students, I looked at him, and I said, "Well, take your shot. Let's hear it."

Tyler pitched me the story, and it was pretty good. I gave him some feedback, and then he said he had another idea. "Let's hear that one," I said. That's when my Spidey senses tingled and fireworks went off in my brain, and I thought, "Yes, this is the one."

I encouraged him to officially submit both projects, but it was the second idea—the one that had caught my attention—that we published. *Janitors* was the first in a five-book series that sold thousands of books, won awards, and helped launch Tyler's career.

I admire Tyler's bravery and willingness to pitch in person, in front of an audience, on command.

Gina Lynn Larsen

Gina had quit writing. She'd been writing and querying her young adult romances for about ten years—as long as we'd been friends—and she had received requests to read her manuscripts, but no one had accepted one yet. Ultimately, Gina decided to set writing down. It wasn't bringing her joy, so she was going to try something new.

I will admit I tried to encourage her to continue writing, but I could tell she was feeling good about moving on to other hobbies, other passions, so I supported her decision.

A few years later, I was hunting hard for some young adult novels to publish. I scoured the slush pile and looked at every single young adult manuscript before narrowing the list down to the top ten. I took them to the editorial team, and we narrowed it down to the top five.

I read fifty pages of each of those five manuscripts and made my recommendations for the top two: a contemporary, issue-driven novel and a historical novel. But what I didn't have was a lighthearted contemporary romantic comedy, and that felt like a miss.

That's when I remembered Gina's manuscript about a girl who gets tricked into kissing her high school crush before finding out it was a joke. I added it to the top three almost on a whim.

The historical novel didn't pan out, so I sent a rejection letter. Between the two that were left, I recommended that we pitch the issue-driven novel because it was more in line with the other YA manuscripts we'd published.

The editorial team heard the pitch, and they said, "This sounds great. The writing is great, the story is great, but what we really want is a story that's more of a lighthearted, contemporary romance at its core."

I said, "You mean like Gina's book?"

"Yes," they said. "Like that."

I emailed Gina and said, "Here's what happened. I kind of pitched your book, and we want to publish it."

"But I'm not writing anymore," she said.

"I know, but we're going to send you a contract anyway."

THERE IS NO ONE RIGHT WAY TO GET PUBLISHED

I share these stories partly to celebrate some excellent books that have found their audiences, that have touched hearts, and that have encouraged imagination, and partly to celebrate friends I've made throughout my career.

But I also want to share them to show that every book takes a different path. There is no one right way to get published. Some of these manuscripts had agents; some of them didn't. Some of them were cold queries; some of them were in-person pitches. Some of them were partial manuscripts that led to full requests. Some of them came about because I made a personal connection with the author before I ever made a connection with the story.

The slush pile can seem like a scary place, but it is also a place where magic happens. Don't be afraid to toss your story into the ring and see what happens.

Just remember that there are aspects of publishing that neither you nor I can control, so do your best to let those things go and give yourself grace.

ONE MORE THING YOU CAN CONTROL

I'm often asked, "What makes a manuscript or a query letter stand out to you?" While there are several answers I could give—many of which are included in this book—when it comes right down to it, a story stands out to me when I can tell that the author loves the story they wrote. There's an emotional connection that I can feel in their writing, and I can tell that the book they have sent to me carries with it a piece of their very self and their very heart. *That's* something I'm looking for.

And that's something only you can do for your story. Only you can tell the story that is inside you.

No two books are the same, and no two authors are the same. No two dreams are the same either. If you don't dream it, no one else will. It's your voice. Don't be afraid to use it.

My advice? Write the book of your heart *from* your heart; the rest will follow.

Chapter 9
Query Letters and Pitching

Query letters can be terrifying. You've written eighty thousand or ninety thousand words, and now you have to sit in front of another blank page and condense all that into two or three paragraphs. Forget even trying to sum it up in one sentence. How can you make it sound interesting and exciting? How can you convince the person reading the query letter—be it agent, editor, or publisher—that they want to read your book?

TEACH ME HOW TO PITCH YOUR BOOK

In many ways, the answer to this last question forms the heart of your pitch, and part of your pitch is to teach me how to talk about your book.

If I like your query letter, then I might like your manuscript. If I do, then I'll need to pitch your story to the other people on the editorial team, to the marketing department, and to the sales team to convince them to offer you a contract. And the best way for me to champion your manuscript is to have a good pitch about the story, which I can get from your query letter.

Story Time with Lisa

Josi S. Kilpack was working on a historical romance about author Sir Walter Scott and his real-life romances, first with his childhood sweetheart, Mina, which ended in heartache, and then with Charlotte Carpenter, who truly captured Walter's heart.

As we were talking about the book around the office, I said, "It's a story of the difference between your first love and your best love." That felt like a good way to summarize the heart of the book, so we put it on the back cover of the ARC. Then, when *Publishers Weekly* reviewed the book, they said this: "A vivid and highly engrossing tale of first love versus best love." Essentially, I taught *Publishers Weekly* how to talk about our book; I told them what I wanted them to say.

That's what I am hoping you can do for me with your query letter.

THE HOOK, THE BOOK, AND THE COOK

A good query letter can truly make or break a submission.

There are three main sections of a query letter, and while they don't have to go in this order, this is the way I remember them: the hook, the book, and the cook. (Thanks to agent Pam Pho, who introduced me to this idea.)

The Hook

A good hook will not only create curiosity, but it will also get me in the right frame of mind to engage with your work in detail. I have only two or three minutes to look at your submission and make a decision, so the goal of the hook is to get me to read the query letter, and the goal of the query letter is to get me to read the first page, and the goal of the first page is to get me to read the whole manuscript.

X + Y Tagline

One way to brainstorm intriguing hooks is to think of it like a movie poster tagline. An "X plus Y" for your comparable stories.

If you've never read *Cujo* by Stephen King, then if I tell you that it's "*Jaws* with paws," you'll probably assume—rightly—that the story will be about a large dog who attacks people.

When James Cameron was pitching the idea of making a movie about the *Titanic*, he said, "It's *Romeo and Juliet* on this boat," and he held up a picture of the ship.

Sometimes it can be as obvious as *Snakes on a Plane*, which is about—surprise!—snakes on a plane.

A really good tagline can even be used as cover copy. On the cover of *Briar Rose* by Jane Yolen, it says, "The bright tale of Sleeping Beauty, the dark tale of the Holocaust, twined together in a story you will never forget." I would never have put those two stories together, which means I am immediately intrigued.

The Girls at the Kingfisher Club by Genevieve Valentine promises a story of "the twelve dancing princesses in the Jazz age." It's a familiar fairy tale but transported into an unexpected time frame.

The tagline for *The Ruins of Lace* by Iris Anthony is "A novel of France, freedom, and forbidden lace." France, I understand; freedom, I understand; but forbidden lace? What's that about?

What are the unique elements of your story, and how can you introduce them in a way that captures my attention?

Comp Titles

Expanding on the tagline, you can also include comp titles to help showcase what makes your book unique, special, or different. Comparative titles are ones similar to yours in tone, theme, writing style, or topic.

I would advise against comparing your manuscript to phenomenon works like Harry Potter or Lord of the Rings; those are once-in-a-generation kinds of stories. Instead, think about what books would sit comfortably next to yours on the shelf. What authors would you like to have lunch with and talk about because your stories have similar viewpoints?

Even though your book may not be a "phenomenon work," you can still draw inspiration from them. For example, instead of saying, "My book is the next Harry Potter," you could say, "Like Harry Potter, my story explores the value of friendship and the necessity of bravery in the face of danger." That way, you're focusing on one element of the story to make the comparison.

The Elevator Pitch

Another kind of hook is called the "elevator pitch" because the theory is that if you are in an elevator with an editor or an agent, you could sum up your book in the time it takes the elevator to reach their floor. (Side note: I would not recommend actually pitching in an elevator unless you are specifically asked to.)

One way to develop this pitch is to see if you can talk about the most interesting aspect of your story in no more than 140 characters—or about a five-second summary.

Story Time with Lisa

The Hourglass Door was released in May 2009, so that summer I spent two hours every Saturday in my local Costco stores trying to sell my book to anybody who walked by. I quickly learned that Saturday Costco shoppers were not there to buy my book. I had maybe three seconds to hand someone a bookmark and say, "I wrote a book," to try to get them to stop and listen to what I had to say. I tried a lot of pitches, and after three months of Saturdays, I settled on the following statement: "It's a love story with a mystery that dates back to Leonardo da Vinci."

That was it. In many cases, that was all I would have time to say, but often, that was all I needed to say because 80 percent of the time, the person would stop, interested for a small heartbeat of a moment.

They would say, "Oh, it's like *The Da Vinci Code*," and I would say, "No, it's nothing like *The Da Vinci Code*." But my pitch worked because now we were in a conversation.

The small sentence I developed was only seventy characters, which meant I could post it on Twitter or put it on a bookmark. It was short and sweet, and I could say it in one breath, instinctively and without hesitation when anybody asked me, "What's your book about?"

Once I had engaged someone in conversation, I could expand on the story and say, "When Abby meets Dante, a foreign exchange student from Italy, her life changes forever. This YA love story has a time-travel twist."

In only 131 characters, I could mention both my main characters, the genre, the audience age group, and a couple of cool details (Italy and time travel).

I'd like to challenge you: Can you write a pitch for your book in fewer than 140 characters?

The Book

Once you've piqued my interest with your hook, the second part of your query letter should tell me the four most important elements about your book: the hero, the goal, the obstacle, and the stakes. (We discussed these back in chapter two.)

The hero. Who is your protagonist? While you don't have to go into deep detail, I do need some information that helps paint a picture of who the person is. Some examples could include:

- Sixteen-year-old Melissa hates her mother.
- As a half-elf, half-orc wizard, William's life isn't easy.
- Florence may have eighty years under her belt, a bad back, bad eyesight, and bad knees, but she isn't going to let that stop her.

You'll notice with these examples that some of them mention the age of the protagonist, which can also point to the audience of the book. A sixteen-year-old character is probably a young adult novel whereas an eighty-year-old character is most likely adult contemporary fiction.

The goal. What does your hero want?

- To recover the stolen amulet of thieving.
- To make it through one day without being laughed at.
- To find a way home.
- To save the world from alien invasion.

Some of these are clearly external goals, while others are internal goals. If you are writing a character-driven story or a coming-of-age story, the goal of wanting to make it through a day without being laughed at can be as compelling as a goal of saving the world.

For the query letter, identify the most important goal, the one that is going to drive your character through the majority of the story. Tell me that.

The obstacles. What is preventing your hero from getting up in the morning and accomplishing the goal that is on their to-do list?

Some examples might include:

- A madman bent on revenge.
- Self-doubt and fear.
- An army of brain-hungry zombies.
- A rival archaeologist searching for the same treasure.

Again, obstacles can be either internal or external. Some of them might be easy to overcome, while others might require a multistep plan in order to accomplish them. You don't have to detail all the obstacles in the query letter, but I'd suggest mentioning at least two or three.

The stakes. What happens if your hero fails to overcome the obstacle?

Here are some examples:

+ Or else all of Middle-earth will fall into shadow.
+ Either she will die, or he will.
+ Will learn the true meaning of Christmas.

How high are the stakes? What is the emotional payoff?

I find that of the four elements, stakes is the one most often neglected in a query letter, yet I think it is the most important of them all. Knowing the stakes motivates me to want to learn more about the story. It offers the promise that the ending is going to make the journey worth it.

One way to articulate the stakes in your book is to write the character's choice at the climactic moment of the plot in the form of a question. Then change it to a statement with a clear "or else this will happen" conclusion.

+ "Móirín has one chance to save Fitz and the Dread Penny Society from the Tempest, and she might have to sacrifice her one chance at love to do so."[1]
+ "Stella must convince her new owners that she can be a new kind of service dog in time to save Cloe's life."[2]
+ "The twins must venture deep into the Cursed Forest to save themselves and their friends. And maybe—just maybe— save the universe from falling into the clutches of the witch in the woods."[3]

Extra elements. Your query letter should also include the title, the word count, and the genre. When it comes to genre, be specific. "Romance" is a massive genre, so drill down and find your subgenre within that category.[4] There's a big difference between Gothic romance, contemporary romance, paranormal romance, and Western romance. Knowing the specific subgenre can help me mentally prepare for that kind of story. It can also help when discussing marketing possibilities and strategies. If we already have several sword-and-sorcery fantasy novels on our schedule, I might be more interested in a query letter that promises an urban fantasy instead.

An Example: *A Brilliant Night of Stars and Ice*

I was scanning titles in the slush pile one day when I saw it: *Carpathia: A Brilliant Night of Stars and Ice* by Rebecca Connolly.

I couldn't click on the link fast enough. Could it be? I grew up reading anything and everything about the *Titanic*, and I was delighted to discover that Rebecca Connolly's query letter held everything I was looking for.

Query Letter

I am seeking publication with Shadow Mountain for my <u>historical novel, CARPATHIA: A BRILLIANT NIGHT OF STARS AND ICE</u>. As a multi-published, bestselling historical romance author, I have built a strong fan base for my works of fiction over the years and my releases continually hit the bestselling Amazon categories. Please see my marketing plan and prior book sales information attached.

Genre & title

CARPATHIA: A BRILLIANT NIGHT OF STARS AND ICE is a <u>72,000-word</u> novel that follows historical figure <u>Arthur Rostron, captain of the *Carpathia*</u>, whose transatlantic voyage is interrupted when they receive a distress call from the *Titanic*. Compelled into action, Rostron orders the *Carpathia* to <u>change course</u>. Rostron races north, through <u>a deadly field of ice</u>, as he pushes his ship to <u>never-before-tested speeds,</u> in an attempt <u>to save</u> <u>the people on board the *Titanic*</u> before it's too late.

Word count

Hero #1

Obstacles

Goal

Obstacle

> What will he find when he gets there, and will his efforts be enough?
>
> Stakes
>
> In alternating chapters, we meet another historical figure—Kate Connolly, an Irish passenger on the *Titanic*. Kate is seeking a better life for herself in America along with two of her friends, but they can only afford third class passage. When the ship hits an iceberg, she and her friends, along with their cabinmate, discover that third class passengers are the last to receive help and instruction. After a harrowing journey up to the boat deck, Kate succeeds in securing a spot on the lifeboat, but surviving may be just as painful as meeting an early end.
>
> Hero #2
> Goal
> Obstacles
> Stakes
>
> The story of the tragedy that beset *Titanic* has been told time and time again, but what of the only ship that headed toward rescue? CARPATHIA: A BRILLIANT NIGHT OF STARS AND ICE is the first historical novel that I know of to be written about Captain Rostron and his heroic crew of men and women. After visiting the *Titanic* Museum in Belfast, I realized there is an important part of history that has yet to be told.
>
> Marketing hook

As good as the query letter was, the manuscript was even better, and I was so excited when we accepted the book for publication and I was able to work with Rebecca on the project.

The Cook

The third part of the query letter is "the cook"—you. I want to know who you are, why you wrote the book, and why I should do business with you.

Some items in this paragraph could include your education or field of study, any writing organizations you belong to (like the Society of Children's Book Writers and Illustrators [SCBWI] or the League of Utah Writers), and if you've won any awards or honors. The caveat, of course, is that I probably don't need to know that you placed third in your elementary school's poetry contest.

I like to know if you've written other books, but you don't necessarily have to tell me their titles. Knowing that you have been published or even that you have other manuscripts you're working on tells me that you're serious about making writing your career.

While your query letter overall is, in essence, a business letter, don't be afraid to show your personality, your voice, or some flair. Maybe you have four cats named after the Beatles. Maybe your favorite place to go on vacation is Disneyland. Maybe you want to highlight a part of the book that will help me understand who you are and get to know you better.

Don't worry if it's your first novel, if you haven't been to any conferences, or if you haven't won any awards. Everybody starts somewhere. A shorter biography paragraph means you can use extra space to tell me more about the plot and subplots of your awesome book. In the end, you can simply say, "This would be my debut novel," and leave it at that if you wish. But you'll be surprised that what you share about yourself can be helpful in a query letter.

THE ART OF THE PITCH

As daunting as it might feel to write a query letter, at least you have time to think about it, write it, and revise it before sharing it. For some people, talking about their story is a different kind of challenge. There will be countless times when you'll need to pitch your book in person, and since you probably don't carry copies of your query letter in your back pocket to whip out and give to anyone who asks about your book, here are some tips about pitching—starting with getting comfortable talking about your book.

Story Time with Lisa

After I wrote *The Hourglass Door*, I knew I was going to have to tell people about it.

That was going to be hard for me because I had essentially written the book in secret. The only people who knew I was writing were the people in my writing group, my husband, my family, and two people at work.

I think I'd kept it a secret because I felt insecure. I wasn't sure if I could do justice to this great idea I had, and I was terrified I would fail. When I finished the manuscript, Chris did something I really appreciated: he removed my name from the submission and ran it through the same review process that every other submission at Shadow Mountain goes through.

And since nobody in the office knew I had written a book, nobody suspected the book was mine. It turned out to be quite nerve-racking because I would be in the lunchroom and someone would say, "Hey, have you heard about this new manuscript Chris is passing around? I think it's called *The Hourglass Door*. It's really good. Have you read it?"

And I would panic and say all in one breath, "Yeah I think I've heard of it but I can't talk about it right now I have to go back to my desk okay thanks bye."

But I knew I was going to have to talk about it eventually, so I started practicing saying, "I wrote a book." I tried to think of it as part of my name: "Hi, I'm Lisa Mangum; I wrote a book. Nice to meet you." The cashier at the grocery store would say, "How was your day?" and I would reply, "Great, I wrote a book." I'd work it into any and all conversation because I needed to be comfortable saying it.

But it's not enough to say, "I wrote a book." Inevitably, the next question is, "What's your book about?"

Tips for Pitching in Person

Your friends might ask you that question in a casual and comfortable setting, but when an editor or an agent asks you the same question at a writing conference, it might suddenly feel like a trick. What if you somehow give the wrong answer?

I've listened to a lot of pitches at a lot of writing conferences, and trust me, there isn't a right or a wrong answer. But there are some do's and don'ts to keep in mind when you are pitching in person.

Let's start with the things *not* to do:

Don't panic. It may feel like the in-person pitch is your one shot at glory and if you mess up, it's over. But it's not like that. The pitch is simply to have a conversation and get to know each other. It's literally so I can hear what your book is about.

Don't panic if the words don't flow as naturally as you might like. The person you are pitching to loves books as much as you do, and we are looking for a book to fall in love with. Why shouldn't it be yours?

Try not to read your pitch from a notebook. I know you're probably nervous, and I don't mind if you have memorized your pitch or have written it down in a notebook that you use as a reference. But often when people read straight from that notebook, they read it too fast, and I miss important details. It can also be hard to get a sense for your personality, which is also something I'm hoping to discover.

Story Time with Lisa

I was holding pitch practice sessions at the Superstars Writing Seminar in Colorado Springs one year when an attendee stopped me between classes and asked if he could practice with me.

"Sure," I said.

He took a deep breath and launched into his pitch. His delivery was stilted, and I could tell he was trying to remember exactly what he had memorized. His summary had all the right elements I was looking for—the hero, the goal, the obstacles, the stakes, the title, the genre—but it didn't have any life to it. It didn't have any personality because he was so nervous about getting the words right.

I let him finish, but instead of giving him feedback on his pitch, I asked, "What's your favorite book?"

"*Ender's Game*," he said.

"Why do you like it?" I asked. "That's not one of my favorite books. What makes it special to you?"

He launched into an explanation of what the story was about and what he loved about it specifically, and he lit up. He was full of passion and enthusiasm. Even his body language changed.

When he was done, I said, "Did you feel the difference when you talked about *Ender's Game* versus when you talked about your book?"

He thought for a minute and said sheepishly, "Yeah."

"So tell me about *your* book," I said. "What's it about?"

This time he told me his story with the same passion and enthusiasm he'd had when talking about *Ender's Game*. It was a much better pitch because he was relaxed, comfortable, and confident.

Whether you're talking to an agent, an editor, a customer, a bookseller, or a friend about your book, be passionate, sincere, and enthusiastic.

Don't watch me read your pitch. On occasion, I've met with people who, rather than telling me what their book is about, simply hand me their pitch and then watch me read it. That is an uncomfortable situation and starts the conversation off on an awkward foot.

Don't take more than your allotted time. If you are participating in pitch sessions at a conference, chances are high the conference has a full schedule of people for the day, which means the editor or agent taking pitches has a lot of people to listen to. If you go over your allotted time, even by just one minute, the cascade effect means that by the time I get to person number five or six or eight, I could be as much as five minutes behind schedule, which means I might not get a break, and that can make it really hard for me to pay attention to the rest of the people pitching.

Don't leave anything behind. Folders, bags, pens, notebooks, water bottles, phones—make sure you take everything with you because if you have to come back, you might be interrupting somebody else's time.

Don't expect a decision or a contract at the end of the pitch. Other editors, publishers, or agents might have a different policy, but for me, I will usually say one of three things: "This sounds like an interesting idea, but I don't think it's right for our publishing house"; "I'd like to see some of your writing style. Please send me three chapters"; or "This sounds amazing! Please send me the full manuscript."

Also, for me, those invitations are open-ended. The rule of thumb is that you should never pitch a project that is not 100 percent complete, but I recognize that once I've requested sample chapters or the full manuscript, an author might want to take a couple of weeks to read the manuscript through one more time. That's fine. Simply make sure that in your query letter, you remind me that we met at a particular conference at a particular time so that "Future Lisa" remembers what "Past Lisa" requested to see.

Here are some things that I do want you to do for an in-person pitch.

Be confident. You have done an amazing thing. You wrote a book. A whole book! With all the words and everything—the adjectives, nouns, verbs, characters, plot, and drama! Be proud of your accomplishment, and be confident in what you have produced. Sit up straight and make eye contact. Your posture and confidence can affect how you present yourself.

Speak slowly and clearly—and loudly—enough that I can hear you. Usually conferences will designate a specific room for pitch sessions, which means that all the editors and agents are together in that enclosed space, at different tables. Once the room is crowded and full and everyone is talking about their books at the same time, the volume can be quite loud.

I recognize that when people get nervous, they often talk fast, so I do my best to ask, "Could you say that one more time? Could you slow down?"

Be friendly. Say hello. Ask me how I'm doing. If you want to ease into a conversation, feel free to tell me what you've learned at the conference or mention a class you attended that you really enjoyed. If you've researched me as an editor or the publishing house I work for, it might be appropriate to mention a title I've worked on or a book you've read that you liked.

Leave time for follow-up questions and conversation. You may only have ten minutes for an in-person pitch with an agent or editor, but that's plenty of time if you only take two minutes for your initial pitch.

I have heard pitches in which the author says, "Okay, in chapter one, we open on . . ." and then they walk me through the entire first chapter, point by point. After nine-and-a-half minutes of a detailed summary, I have to say, "I'm sorry, but our time is up."

I want to give feedback on what I think about your story. I want to ask questions about your characters or dig deeper into a subplot or ask about your writing process. Let's talk!

Have another idea in your back pocket. You might not need to use it, but I've heard plenty of pitches that I could tell right away weren't going to be a good fit for our publishing house. In those cases, I try to immediately ask, "Are you working on anything else?" because perhaps *that* idea is one I'm interested in.

Because pitching can be conversational, you might not use all the tools in every situation. If you are prepared with a compelling hook, if you feel comfortable talking about the four main elements of your story, if you have a couple of comps you can reference, you'll be in good shape to navigate any conversation you find yourself in.

Story Time with Lisa

My class on queries and pitching was the first session of the first day of the writing conference. At the end of the class, I told the attendees I wanted them to keep track of how many people they pitched their book to over the weekend, then email me that number. I would edit the query letter of whoever had the highest number. I thought the contest would be a fun way to get everybody talking about their book and give them some good pitch practice over the weekend.

After lunch, a woman came up to me and said, "You ruined my life."

Taken aback, I said, "I'm so sorry. What happened?"

"I was in your class about pitching this morning," she said, clearly upset, "and I have been talking to every single person about my book today, and it's not working."

"I have a break right now," I said. "Let's sit down, and you can tell me your pitch. Maybe I can help you with it." We sat on a bench in the hallway, and I asked my standard opening question, "What's your book about?"

She explained that it was a historical novel about the people building the transcontinental railroad through a small town in Missouri. After about three or four minutes of background and summary, I tried to sum up the conversation. "Okay," I said, "so your book is about the transcontinental railroad, and—"

She slapped her hands on her legs and said, "No! It's about a girl who is trying to decide whether she should go back east to pursue her dream of being a doctor or if she should stay in her hometown and marry the boy next door."

I sat there for what felt like a very long time before I said, "*That* is your pitch."

She had gotten so caught up in trying to establish the setting that she had missed the fact she could actually sum up her book perfectly by explaining the choice her main character had to make: become a doctor or marry the boy next door?

"Stop talking about the train," I said gently. "You don't need to mention the train."

Then she said, "I can't figure out how to do the X plus Y tags. And I don't know what my comps should be."

"Then don't use them."

She paused. "But in your class—"

"I know. But if you can't come up with a really good tagline or comps right now, don't worry about it. If you're bad at writing a one-paragraph hook that includes the hero, the goal, the obstacles, and stakes, set it aside and come back to it. Practice it later. Use the tools where and when it makes sense."

I talked with her about her story for another twenty minutes, helping her streamline the pitch and draw out the most interesting details. Then I sent her on her way.

The next day, she found me, and unlike the thundercloud from the day before, she was all sunshine and smiles. "I've been practicing my new pitch," she said, "and everybody loves it."

I was so happy to hear that, partly because she'd been really angry with me the day before, but mostly because I was grateful that she'd found the confidence to talk about her book in a comfortable and compelling way.

NOW HIRING!

I sometimes joke that I'm simply looking for a story that can sell 100,000 copies, and while there is a kernel of truth to that, the deeper truth is that I'm looking for people whom I can work with and who will help market and support their book.

- I'm looking for a writer with imagination, who can deliver amazing and original stories regularly and on time.
- I'm looking for a writer with vision, who can see how they fit into the overall publishing world.
- I'm looking for a writer who is flexible and can roll with the inevitable punches that come with the industry.
- I'm looking for a writer who can speak passionately about their work and inspire people to buy their books.

Does that sound like you? Then, I'm looking for *you*!

Chapter 10
Quit. But If You Can't . . .

Writing is hard.

Learning how to write is hard too.

If you are feeling overwhelmed by it all, I get it. It's a lot.

And if you are thinking that you made a mistake by even trying to be a writer because—you know—you clearly don't know anything about writing and everything you thought you knew about writing was wrong and everyone else seems so close to reaching their goals while you're still trying to figure out where the commas go, well, I get that too.

Sometimes it seems like being an author is pure folly. Sometimes it seems like the path is lined with more pitfalls than primroses. Like everything and everyone is out to get you. And rejection hurts; it always will—there's no way around that.

Maybe here at the end of this book you feel sad and lost and like you should just give up. Like maybe the story you once loved doesn't love you back.

Trust me—you're in good company.

We've all felt "Impostor Syndrome"—I experienced it while writing this book—and it's a beast.

Sometimes I'll be on a panel with another editor or agent, and they'll say they have ten or fifteen years of experience, and I'll feel a sense of awe, like, "Wow! That's a long time!" And then the little voice in the back of my head chimes in and says, "Yes, that is a long time. But you have more than twenty-five years of experience. You're doing okay."

But it's hard to shake the feeling of doubt and insecurity.

Story Time with Lisa

After writing and publishing a couple of nonfiction books, Dennis called me up, saying he had an idea for a novel about a flight attendant who ends up working a route that takes her to Area 51—where the aliens live, naturally. He was excited about it, so being the good sister, I went over to his house to talk about his story, his plot, and his characters. As we talked more about Gina, the flight attendant, and Reggie, one of the aliens on her route, Dennis suddenly looked at me with horror in his eyes and said, "Wait—am I writing a rom-com?"

And I laughed and laughed and laughed and said, "Yes, you are. Well, actually you're writing more of a *com*-rom—more comedy than romance." That seemed to help calm him down.

Now that he's elbow-deep into writing the story, he'll call or text me regularly from what we lovingly call "the ledge."

> DENNIS: Why is it that it is so much easier to look at someone else's story, and know how to fix/improve it, than it is to do that with my own story???
>
> ME: Because you still have Creative Brain turned on when you are looking at your own stuff. Editor Brain comes later. Have you run into a problem that needs help from Story Lisa?
>
> DENNIS: Not a huge one, other than my usual "WHERE DO I GO FROM HERE, AND WHAT IF MY STORY

IS SECRETLY STUPID AND I'M A NO-TALENT
HACK?" If it's Wednesday, it must be the ledge.
Me: Ah, the song of my people . . .

Impostor syndrome is normal, and it will pass. (Even though it's the pits while you are wading through it.)

No matter if you are published or unpublished, no matter if you write fiction or nonfiction, no matter if you are just starting out or if you have books in the double-digits under your belt—*you are a writer*. And that matters.

THE BEST ADVICE

Years ago, I was attending a writing conference when my friend Rick Walton stood up to speak. He was a professor at the local college and much beloved by students and faculty alike. He was a writer and creator and genuinely good person, and the question came up: "What advice do you have for new writers?"

He looked out over that group of brand-new, bright-eyed, hopeful writers, and he said, "Quit."

I could both hear and *feel* the low murmur that passed through the crowd.

And then he said, "But if you can't"—long pause—"do the work."

I've always remembered what he said and how he said it, because there are so many things we could be doing with our time besides writing—valuable things, important things, silly, inconsequential things. There are so many demands on your time that if writing doesn't bring you joy and fulfillment, if it doesn't fill you with courage or purpose, then, guess what? It's okay to quit. It's okay to set the book down, set the laptop down, set the pen and paper down and walk away. It's fine.

But if you *can't* do that, if there is something inside you that won't let you walk away from that story or from those words, then you have to do the work. It's the only way through it.

WHY DO YOU WRITE?

Every so often, I come across a submission in the slush pile that I remember. *The Rainbow Zebra* was a five-page story about a rainbow zebra who feels bad that he doesn't have black-and-white stripes like all the other zebras. He runs away, then the other zebras apologize to him, and he comes home. All the zebras become friends and play badminton together. The end.

The story was written and illustrated by an eight-year-old girl who "wanted to make a book that people could read. I wanted to help people have fun when they read." (Mission accomplished, Miss Ruby. Mission accomplished.)

Why do *you* write?

To be published? To tell a story? To become rich and famous? To preserve your history? To be happy?

There are no wrong answers to this question, but there is an answer that is unique to you, and that answer might change over the course of your career as a writer. It's important to find the right answer *for you*—to set your own goals and define your own success. If you feel that success looks like a #1 spot on the *New York Times* bestseller list, your path is going to be different from someone else's whose success is perhaps just finishing a problematic chapter.

There are as many steps along the path of success as there are books in the bookstore, and not everybody's success will look the same, just as not everybody's answer to why they write will look exactly the same. That's okay.

Writing is solitary—it's just you, your brain, and your pages— and sometimes it's really nice to be around other writers who are on the same path with you, who are traveling the same journey you are, and who can help you when you stumble and celebrate with you when you succeed.

I'm a big believer in celebrating success, especially when it comes to writing. It can take months or years of hard work before you feel good about what you've got on paper, but that doesn't mean you shouldn't celebrate the milestones along the way. Don't wait until you have achieved what you think is your end goal before you celebrate.

Maybe you reward yourself when you hit a certain word count, reach a certain number of chapters, or write for a certain number of days in a row. Whatever your goal is, take time to celebrate when you accomplish it, even if it's giving yourself a round of applause or a pat on the back. Celebrate every day that you get words on a page or unravel a knotty problem in your head or come up with a new idea. Creation should be joyful.

MEMORABLE FIRSTS

Think back to some of your memorable firsts:

- The first story you wrote in elementary school.
- The first creative writing class you took.
- The first time you finished a manuscript.
- The first time you were published.

Have you ever gone back to one of those first milestones? An earlier draft of a project? Or a story you worked on years ago? Did you find yourself cringing at the mistakes you found there? I did with mine. But I have also smiled because those mistakes are evidence of how much I have grown. It is important to look ahead at your goals but to also look back at the progress you have made.

I love this quote from Tracy Hickman: "I have not yet written my best book."[1]

Notice that he didn't say that his previous work was *bad* or *worthless*. He's saying that there is always more to learn. There is always growth to be gained. He still has the potential to write his *best book ever.*

If you are still working toward some of those firsts, great! All firsts and all improvements are worth celebrating.

BE HOPEFUL

My mom has been gone for several years now, and I think about her all the time. Especially whenever I use a paper clip.

We used to joke that when God was organizing families, He grouped a bunch of people together, but when the conversation turned to a lengthy and in-depth discussion about office supplies, everyone but me and Mom left, so God said, "Well, clearly you two *have* to be family."

Here's what I love about paper clips. Sure, they are small, but they have a really important job: they bring things together and keep them safe. And if you have enough of them, you can link them into a really cool chain.

Hope is the same way, I think. It brings people together; it can keep us safe. And when we share our hope with each other, it becomes a chain linking us together in the best way possible.

After Mom passed away, I started noticing paper clips in my path whenever I was sad and needed a hug from my mom or when I was undertaking a big project and needed someone to whisper in my ear, "You can do it."

These days, paper clips are my personal symbol of hope, a sign that Mom really isn't that far away, that she's looking out for me, and that we are still connected—together and safe.

My mom always believed that the story I had to tell was a story worth telling. She always told me that I could do anything.

I think about what she taught me all the time. About the legacy of hope that she left me. Hope is hard to quantify with a number, but as Sam Winchester says, "Hope's kinda the whole point."[2]

BE GENTLE

I was on a panel once when we were all asked to give our best writing advice, and while I have some stock answers that have served me well in such situations, that day, the words that came out of my mouth were, "Be gentle with yourself and your time."

I worry that sometimes we put these restrictions on our time that ultimately may cause us more stress than encouragement. The industry we have all chosen to embrace is filled with deadlines and internal and external roadblocks, so be gentle with yourself when your writing takes time. Be gentle with yourself as you spend time looking for an agent, finding a publisher, actually getting published, writing another book, or any of the other thousand necessities that this profession seems to demand of us.

Yes, there are twenty-four hours in a day, but there is only one *you*, which makes you, as the creative storyteller, extraordinarily valuable.

If you need to take time to rest—do it. If you need to spend time caring for your family—do it.

So much of writing—and life—is about balance. Imagine a scale with a sizable weight on one side and very little weight on the other. It'd be pretty clear that the scale is out of balance and that there are only two ways to fix it.

One: you sacrifice something from one side to reduce the weight overall and align the plates. Sure, that works, but it means you have to give up things you love or things that are helpful. You give up time for yourself or time with your family. You give up going to the movies. You give up exercise or sleep.

Two: you move weights from one side to the other until they are even. That works, too, but it doesn't actually reduce your workload. You've simply shifted it from one place to another, and that can be even more stressful than living a life that isn't in balance.

Maybe the more helpful image isn't a scale but an equalizer—like for music. Everything has its place and is important, and your goal is to keep things in harmony.

Sometimes finding the perfect balance is about volume. Perhaps you are in a phase of your life where you can devote a lot of time to writing, and you can turn the volume up really loud, but that doesn't mean you have to silence the other channels. They are still there, providing the backbeat to your projects.

And later, maybe you'll need to turn down the volume on your writing because you need to turn up the volume on your family or your work. That's okay, too, because the words that fill you are still there—and they will still be there when you get back.

It's okay to lower the volume when the noise gets to be too loud.

Try to think less about sacrifice and stress and more about keeping your connections to what you value strong and unencumbered.

Be gentle with yourself and your time.

BE BOLD

Years ago, I read an article about editing, and while I'd love to cite my source, I don't remember the author, yet I clearly remember the advice because it has stuck with me for decades: "Be bold enough to edit in ink."

Oh, how I, as a young editor starting to wade into the shallow end of the publishing pool, wanted to be that bold. Imagine the confidence it takes to pick up a pen and say, "This. Right here. This is wrong. And I will make it right."

And not because I *thought* I knew. But because I *knew*.

Because I was *right*.

I often use my red pen as a finely honed scalpel, excising problems with a flick of my wrist. Sometimes I use it like a sledgehammer, leveling mountains of prose with ease.

But I like to use it most as a magic wand because it allows me to bring something into existence that wasn't there before. Something better. Something stronger.

My goal as an editor and as a writer is to add perspective and clarity to a story.

When you or I are writing the story of our lives, I hope we can be bold enough to "write it in ink."

Grab your own red pen and edit out your self-doubt, your fears, your worry, your secret belief that you're an impostor and that the Story Police will one day show up on your doorstep and say, "I'm sorry, but it's come to our attention that you are writing stories, and, well, that just isn't allowed for the likes of you." (Spoiler Alert: There is no such organization as the Story Police, so keep on writing whatever you want, as often as you want.)

Use that red pen, and be bold enough to find those spots in your own story where you can create more choices. Write COURAGE in all caps whenever you need it. Add hope to every word, every line, every paragraph, every page that you live.

Most of all, be bold enough to ask for help.

How Did I Get Here?

A number of years ago, Kevin J. Anderson invited me to be an instructor at the Superstars Writing Seminar. I have a photo from 2017 of a panel filled with six *New York Times* best-selling authors: Dave Farland, Jody Lynn Nye, Jim Butcher, Rebecca Moesta, Kevin J. Anderson, and Todd McCaffrey. Alongside those authors are Mark Lefebvre, founder of Kobo Writing Life; James Artemis Owen, an internationally renowned artist and storyteller; and Claire Eddy, senior editor at TOR.

And then there's me.

When I look at that photo, I ask myself, "How did I get here? How did I end up sitting on a panel with such talent, such influence? I just feel like little ol' me, who works at a midsized regional publishing house and who wrote some books—how did I get *here*?"

Remember that letter I got from Madeleine Robins at TOR back in 1992?

I shared that story in 2017, sitting next to Claire Eddy, and she told me the other half of the story.

She said that way back in the 1980s, Tom Doherty, founder of TOR Books and a legend in the publishing industry, decided to continue a tradition begun by Bennet Cerf from Random House, that if a young person wrote to the publishing company asking for advice or help, someone would write back.

That means, in the early 1980s, when young Lisa was devouring books at a breakneck pace, discovering epic fantasy for the first time and falling in love with words and story, a policy was put into place that was still being upheld years later when high school Lisa wrote to TOR, asking for help.

(In a perfect story, Claire would have been the one to have written me back, just for literary symmetry, but alas, real life isn't always as neat and tidy as fiction is.)

The reason I was on that panel next to those authors and editors was that eighteen-year-old Lisa had been bold enough to write to the publisher of her favorite books and say, "I want to do what you do. Show me the way."

I still have the letter Madeleine sent me. I keep it, in part because after I started working full time as an editor, I made a promise to myself that if I was ever in a position to do for someone else what Madeleine did for me, I would do it. It is the reason my personal motto over the years has been "I will do my best to help anyone who asks."

The help you need is out there. People are ready to help you. They want to help you. You just have to be bold enough to ask for it. Then be bold enough to follow that path.

The truth is we are all in a position to help each other. You may think that you don't have anything to give because you are at the beginning stages of your journey. You haven't published anything, won any awards, or finished a manuscript. That doesn't matter; you are still in a position to help someone next to you who is on the same journey.

To quote the last two lines of the poem "The Summer Day" by Mary Oliver:

> *Tell me, what is it you plan to do*
> *with your one wild and precious life?*[3]

You have the skills. You have the knowledge. You can do The Thing.

BE BRAVE

When I was younger, I was paralyzingly shy. I never wanted to be the center of attention. I didn't like to talk to people or talk in front of people. I rarely spoke up in class, even when I knew the answer. And forget about doing something as public as *singing*—even if I was just one of an entire group of kids.

No, I was perfectly happy to stay in the library instead of going to school dances, thank you very much.

Unsurprisingly, I found it easy to fall into the stories I read in books or watched on TV. As I grew up, I enjoyed many great shows, but it wasn't until 2016 that I found my *favorite* show ever: *Supernatural.*

I started watching it in September, and I watched the first eleven seasons in thirty-three days. (Yeah. Big fan.)

Fifteen months later—January 2018—I was starting my sixth time through the series when I decided to undertake a project wherein I would analyze each episode for plot, character, and theme as well as identify a helpful writing tip.

My plan was to simply highlight one interesting note about the episode, maybe mention the theme, and be done in a few hundred words. But as with most projects we are passionate about, it quickly took on a life of its own.

Then my cat Allie died. Then my mother-in-law died.

I came to rely more and more on my time with the Winchesters to get me through the hard times. Watch. Write. Repeat.

From January to July, I generated more than 450,000 words on my project.

And then in August, my mother died. My mom, who had taught me to read, who had taught me to write, who had taught me to edit . . .

On Saturday afternoon, she was sick. By Tuesday morning, she was gone.

And the Winchesters were about the only thing keeping me going. Somehow, a story about two brothers taking on all the monsters in the world and prevailing against them gave me the courage to face the challenges in my world and find a way to prevail.

Throughout my grief, I continued to watch and rewatch the show until in March 2020, I attended a *Supernatural* convention in Las Vegas with some friends.

On Friday afternoon, my friend Victoria said, "Hey, we should do karaoke tonight. What do you think?"

I hesitated.

I had a VIP pass for the convention, and my VIP coordinator had literally texted: "Does anyone want to sing at karaoke? Please let me know."

Toss my name in the ring and risk being in front of all those people? Why would I? Plus, I have never been a singer, and I had spent years being afraid of getting on a stage.

But I had also spent years watching my Winchester boys be brave and bold and fearless.

With a wild rush of bravery surging through me, I told Victoria, "I think you should choose your next words carefully because if you want to do karaoke, we *will* do karaoke. Guaranteed."

We looked at each other, agreed that we were crazy to even consider it, and then, before either of us could change our minds, I replied to the text: "I'd like to sing a song with my friend Victoria. (It will be very bad, as I can't actually sing.)"

I wanted to do it partly because I wanted to create a memory with my friends but mostly because I wanted to be a part of a story I loved. The chance to be on stage with some of the cast from the show? I wasn't going to let a little sting of fear stop me.

That's not to say I wasn't unspeakably nervous walking into the ballroom that night. Was I really going to do this? Was I really going to get on stage and sing "Livin' on a Prayer" by Bon Jovi in front of more than 2,000 people?

My friend Lynn said, "It's not about whether or not you can sing. It's about your energy. Just have fun with it."

Right before the party started, I looked down, and there on the carpet was a single silver paper clip. "Hi, Mom," I whispered, tucking the clip into my pocket.

Then Victoria and I took the stage (not first, thankfully!), and well . . .

I remember the feeling of joyous abandon that filled me as the music started. And I remember the moment when I looked around the stage, at the ballroom, at all my friends and the people in the crowd who loved the same story I did—the story we were all part of—and thought, *Not bad for a shy little girl who used to be terrified to sing in public.*

I share this story because I want you to feel brave enough to use your voice.

Yes, it can be scary to have people looking at you while you try something new or attempt something that's maybe not in your primary skill set. But remember this as you tuck that paper clip of hope into your pocket: you are surrounded by friends who love the same things you love, who want to see you succeed. The energy you put toward your adventures counts. Everything counts.

And there is so much joy to be had in just having fun with it—in being brave enough to *try* it, in being brave enough to make your voice heard.

Writing is powerful all on its own, but *sharing* it heightens its intensity. I hope you feel brave enough to share your story with someone—even if that someone is simply you.

Write down how you feel, what you did, what you learned, what you hope for, and then invite us to experience that with you. Tell us your truth. Invite us into your story.

And perhaps later, when you hear "Livin' on a Prayer," you'll think about a shy little girl who grew up to be brave enough to use her voice—and how you can use the power of *your* voice to influence others for good.

PERMISSION GRANTED

If you still feel like you need permission to be a writer, then from me to you, you have my permission to be prolific. Write as many books as you want, write short stories and poetry and screenplays and novellas, and write in every genre you want to write in.

You have my permission to be patient. Publishing is a long game. It takes a long time to write a book, and it takes a long time to get it edited, and then to find an agent, and then to get it published, and then to get it on the shelf. Be patient with yourself through the process.

You have my permission to be persistent. Be persistent in learning and honing your craft. Be persistent in digging out the ideas from the world around you and polishing them until they shine like nothing we've seen before.

When my mom said to me, "You can do this"—I believed her.

And because I believed her, I wrote this book so I could tell *you*: You can do this. I believe in you.

I hope you believe in you too.

Be hopeful. Be gentle. Be bold. And be brave.

ONE LAST THING

Remember that dream I asked you to come up with at the beginning of this book? I'd like you to raise your hand as high as you can. (Yes, I know you might be in a public place, or maybe you are home alone—it doesn't matter; just do it.) Good. Now, reach a little higher. Did you do it? Did you feel it—that lift, that stretch?

Did you know you had that extra bit of magic inside you?

Now imagine that your dream is right there, waiting just at the edge of your fingertips. Reach out—and then reach a little higher—and claim it, make it your own. Make it come true.

Acknowledgments

This book took me twenty-six days—and twenty-six years—to write. I couldn't have done it without my friends and family, who have been with me every step of the way.

To Mom and Dad. You are both gone now, but the love you gave me and what you taught me will live inside me forever. I am who I am because of you.

To Dennis. Thank you for being the best brother in the world. You always know how to lift me or make me laugh—often at the same time. Next time we journey to the Dragon Town Hall, drinks are on me. Also, "I say we take off and nuke the entire site from orbit. It's the only way to be sure." (I couldn't *not* have this *Aliens* quote in the book.)

To Tracy. You have been by my side for more than half my life. Thank you for filling my Adventure Book with the best memories.

Thanks to my delightful and careful editor, Samantha Millburn. It was probably a little weird editing a book by another editor, but you made the process easy for me. Thanks for being my cheerleader and for not laughing at my copyediting mistakes.

Special thanks to the rest of my Shadow Mountain family: Chris Schoebinger, Heidi Gordon, Callie Hansen, Derk Koldewyn, Troy Butcher, Haley Haskins, Bri Cornell, Amy Parker, Ashley Olson, Lehi Quiroz, Garth Bruner, Heather Ward, Rachael Ward,

Breanna Anderl, Halle Ballingham, Ali Nelson, Allison Mathews, and Jessica Guernsey.

When you end up working for the same company for more than two decades, your path crosses those of many people. To my past colleagues, Jay Parry and Jack Lyon. I could not have learned the craft of editing and publishing from two better men. To Cory Maxwell and Jana Erickson, whose kindness and encouragement set my feet firmly on this path all those years ago. Much love to Emily Watts, Tracy Keck, Kristen Evans, Richard Erickson, Kayla Hackett, Shauna Gibby, Janna DeVore, Jill Schaugaard, Julia McCracken, Sarah Cobabe, Karen Zelnick Rivera, Michelle Moore, Gary Garff, Jennifer Adams, Amy Stewart, Malina Grigg, Leslie Stitt, Laurie Cook, Sheryl Dickert Smith, Tonya Facemyer, Richard Peterson, George Bickerstaff, and Suzanne Brady.

I am so lucky to have made countless wonderful friends through the many writing conferences I've attended or taught at. If we've ever said hi at Superstars Writing Seminar, LTUE, Storymakers, WIFYR, Realm Makers, ANWA, League of Utah Writers, Teen Author Boot Camp, The Teen Writer's Conference, Book Academy, FyreCon, Writing for Charity, or Apex Writer's Group, I wrote this book for all of you.

Thank you all for being part of my story and for letting me be part of yours.

Recommended Resources

General Writing Guides

American Night Writers Association. *Create, Craft, Critique, and More: A Guide to the Many Facets of Writing.*

Atchity, Kenneth. *A Writer's Time: Making the Time to Write. 2nd Revised Ed.*

Block, Lawrence. *The Liar's Bible: A Good Book for Fiction Writers.*

Klinkenborg, Verlyn. *Several Short Sentences About Writing.*

Koontz, Dean. *How to Write Best Selling Fiction.*

LaPlante, Alice. *The Making of a Story: A Norton Guide to Creative Writing.*

Maass, Donald. *The Emotional Craft of Fiction: How to Write the Story Beneath the Surface.*

———. *Writing the Breakout Novel: Insider Advice for Taking Your Fiction to the Next Level.*

Moon, Wulf. *How to Write a Howling Good Story.*

Obstfeld, Raymond. *Fiction First Aid: Instant Remedies for Novels and Stories.*

Ostrom, Hans, Wendy Bishop, and Katharine Haake. *Metro: Journeys in Writing Creatively.*

Penn, Joanna. *Writing the Shadow: Turn Your Inner Darkness into Words.*

Phillips, Melanie Anne, and Chris Huntley. *Dramatica: A New Theory of Story.*

Pinkston, Tristi. The Write It Right series.

Provost, Gary. *100 Ways to Improve Your Writing: Proven Professional Techniques for Writing with Style and Power.*

Shoemaker, Martin L. *Making Story Models: Tools for Visualizing Your Story.*

Suede, Damon. *Verbalize: Bring Stories to Life and Life to Stories.*

Williams, Joseph M. *Style: Ten Lessons in Clarity and Grace.*

Zuckerman, Albert. *Writing the Blockbuster Novel. Revised and Updated.*

Specific Writing Topics

Essoe, Joshua. *Action Sequences & Sex Scenes.*

———. *Worldbuilding & Mood and Atmosphere.*

Hoch, Carla. *Fight Write: How to Write Believable Fight Scenes.*

Kenyon, Sherrilyn. *The Character Naming Sourcebook.*

Osborne, Jon R. *World Building for Novices.*

Thom, James Alexander. *Once upon a Time It Was Now: The Art and Craft of Writing Historical Fiction.*

VanderMeer, Jeff. *Wonderbook: The Illustrated Guide to Creating Imaginative Fiction.*

Character Development

Black, Sacha. *13 Steps to Evil: How to Craft Superbad Villains.*

Card, Orson Scott. *Elements of Fiction Writing: Character & Viewpoint.*

Carlson, Michael J. *Hurting Your Characters: A Writer's Guide to Describing Injuries and Pain from the Character's Point of View.*

Dixon, Debra. *GMC: Goal, Motivation, and Conflict.*

Weiland, K. M. *Creating Character Arcs: The Masterful Author's Guide to Uniting Story Structure, Plot, and Character Development.*

Memoir and Inspiration

Jovin, Ellen. *Rebel with a Clause: Tales and Tips from a Roving Grammarian.*

King, Stephen. *On Writing: A Memoir of the Craft.*

Lamott, Anne. *Bird by Bird: Some Instructions on Writing and Life.*

Lerner, Betsy. *The Forest for the Trees: An Editor's Advice to Writers.*

Mandeville, Chris. *52 Ways to Get Unstuck: Exercises to Break Through Writer's Block.*

Morrell, David. *The Successful Novelist: A Lifetime of Lessons About Writing and Publishing.*

Pressfield, Steven. *Do the Work: Overcome Resistance and Get Out of Your Own Way.*

———. *Turning Pro: Tap Your Inner Power and Create Your Life's Work.*

———. *The War of Art: Break Through the Blocks and Win Your Inner Creative Battles.*

Rhodes, Richard. *How to Write: Advice and Reflections.*

Rogers, Bruce Holland. *Word Work: Surviving and Thriving as a Writer.*

Syme, Becca. *Dear Writer, Are You in Burnout?*

Syme, Becca, and Susan Bischoff. *Dear Writer, Are You Intuitive?*

Webb, William Alan, and Chris Kennedy. *Brief Lessons in Writing.*

Plot and Story Structure

Bell, James Scott. *Plot & Structure: Techniques and Exercises for Crafting a Plot That Grips Readers from Start to Finish.*

Block, Lawrence. *Writing the Novel from Plot to Print to Pixel: Expanded and Updated.*

Booker, Christopher. *The Seven Basic Plots: Why We Tell Stories.*

Brody, Jessica. *Save the Cat! Writes a Novel.*

Brooks, Larry. *Story Engineering: Mastering the 6 Core Competencies of Successful Writing.*

Burroway, Janet. *Writing Fiction: A Guide to Narrative Craft.*

Chester, Deborah. *The Fantasy Fiction Formula.*

Cron, Lisa. *Story Genius: How to Use Brain Science to Go Beyond Outlining and Write a Riveting Novel (Before You Waste Three Years Writing 327 Pages That Go Nowhere).*

Farland, David. *Million Dollar Outlines.*

Hayes, Gwen. *Romancing the Beat: Story Structure for Romance Novels.*

Ikenberry, Kevin. *The Mercenary Guide to Story Structure.*

Ingermanson, Randy. *How to Write a Novel Using the Snowflake Method.*

McKee, Robert. *Story: Substance, Structure, Style, and the Principles of Screenwriting.*

Schechter, Jeffrey. *My Story Can Beat up Your Story: Ten Ways to Toughen up Your Screenplay from Opening Hook to Knockout Punch.*

Snyder, Blake. *Save the Cat! The Last Book on Screenwriting You'll Ever Need.*

Vogler, Christopher. *The Writer's Journey: Mythic Structure for Writers.*

Editing

Bills, Suzy. *The Freelance Editor's Handbook: A Complete Guide to Making Your Business Thrive.*

Browne, Renni. *Self-Editing for Fiction Writers, 2nd ed.: How to Edit Yourself into Print.*

Einsohn, Amy, and Marilyn Schwartz. *The Copyeditor's Handbook and Workbook.*

Garner, Bryan A. *Garner's Modern English Usage.*

Hickman, Kirt. *Revising Fiction: Making Sense of the Madness. The Comprehensive and Practical Guide to Self-Editing.*

McLendon, Lisa. *The Perfect English Grammar Workbook: Simple Rules and Quizzes to Master Today's English.*

Norton, Scott. *Developmental Editing.*

Saller, Carol Fisher. *The Subversive Copy Editor.*

Schneider, Amy J. *The Chicago Guide to Copyediting Fiction.*

The University of Chicago Press Editorial Staff. *The Chicago Manual of Style, 18th edition.*

Trask, R. L. *The Penguin Guide to Punctuation.*

Walsh, Bill. *Lapsing into a Comma: A Curmudgeon's Guide to the Many Things That Can Go Wrong in Print—and How to Avoid Them.*

Yin, Karen. *The Conscious Style Guide: A Flexible Approach to Language That Includes, Respects, and Empowers.*

Notes

Introduction: So You Want to Write a Book

1. Anne Rockwell, *The Awful Mess* (New York: Parents' Magazine Press, 1973), 6–7.

Chapter 1: Starting the Story

1. Shannon Hale (@haleshannon), X, August 27, 2015, 8:27 a.m., https://twitter.com/haleshannon/status/636907891379736576?lang=en.

2. See National Institutes of Health, "Enzyme Enhances, Erases Long-Term Memories in Rats," March 3, 2011, https://www.nih.gov/news-events/news-releases/enzyme-enhances-erases long-term-memories-rats.

3. See Britannica, s.v. "Zombie-Ant Fungus," last modified March 7, 2023, https://www.britannica.com/science/zombie-ant-fungus.

4. See "Natural Radioactivity in Food," United States Environmental Protection Agency, accessed March 30, 2024, https://www.epa.gov/radtown/natural-radioactivity-food.

5. See Corrie Goldman, "This Is Your brain on Jane Austen, and Stanford Researchers Are Taking Notes," Stanford Arts, September 7, 2012. https://arts.stanford.edu/this-is-your-brain-on-jane-austen-and-stanford-researchers-are-taking-notes/.

6. Wikipedia, s.v. "Hero's Journey," last modified March 29, 2024, 10:17, https://en.wikipedia.org/wiki/Hero%27s_journey.

7. Matthew Winkler and Kirill Yeretsky, "The Hero's Journey According to Joseph Campbell—Video by Matthew Winkler and

Kirill Yeretsky," YouTube video, 3:09, August 22, 2016, https://www.youtube.com/watch?v=d1Zxt28ff-E.

8. "How to Write Three Act Structure," MasterClass, last modified September 2, 2021, https://www.masterclass.com/articles/how-to-write-three-act-structure.

9. See "How to Use Seven-Point Story Structure in Your Writing," MasterClass, last modified July 28, 2021, https://www.masterclass.com/articles/how-to-use-seven-point-story-structure-in-your-writing.

10. Randy Ingermanson, "The Snowflake Method for Designing a Novel," Advanced Fiction Writing, accessed March 30, 2024, https://www.advancedfictionwriting.com/articles/snowflake-method/.

11. See Wikipedia, s.v. "Scene and Sequel," last modified September 3, 2023, 01:46, https://en.wikipedia.org/wiki/Scene_and_sequel.

12. See Wikipedia, s.v. "Blake Snyder," last modified March 20, 2024, 13:38, https://en.wikipedia.org/wiki/Blake_Snyder.

13. Kevin Ikenberry, *The Mercenary Guide to Story Structure* (Coinjock, NC: Quillcraft Press, 2022).

14. Nancy Kress, "6 Tips to Choosing the Right Point of View," *Writers Digest*, March 11, 2008, https://www.writersdigest.com/writing-articles/6-tips-to-choosing-the-right-point-of-view.

15. Lisa Mangum, *After Hello* (Salt Lake City: Shadow Mountain, 2012), 1.

16. Mangum, *After Hello*, 7.

17. See Donald Maass, *Writing the Breakout Novel Workbook* (New York: Writer's Digest Books, 2004), 8-13.

18. Stephen King, *The Gunslinger. Revised and Expanded Throughout* (New York: Plume, 1982, 2003), 3.

19. Neil Gaiman, *The Graveyard Book* (New York: HarperCollins, 2008), 2.

20. M. M. Kaye, *The Far Pavilions* (New York: Bantam Books, 1978), 1.

21. Russell Hoban, *Riddley Walker, Extended Edition* (Bloomington, IN: Indiana University Press, 1980, 1998), 1.

22. Margaret Atwood, *Oryx and Crake* (New York: Doubleday, 2003), 3.

23. Margaret Atwood, *The Blind Assassin* (New York: Doubleday, 2000), 1.

24. Tad Williams, *Otherland, Vol. 1: City of Golden Shadow* (New York: DAW Books, 1996), 1.

25. Toni Morrison, *Beloved* (New York: Plume, 1987), 3.

26. Peter Lefcourt, *Di and I* (New York: HarperPerennial, 1995), xi.

27. Robin McKinley, *Sunshine* (New York: Berkley Books, 2003), 3.

28. Neal Stephenson, *Anathem* (New York: Harper, 2008), 3.

29. Dante Alighieri, *The Divine Comedy: Inferno*, trans. Allen Mandelbaum (New York: Bantam Books, 1980), 59.

30. Patrick Rothfuss, *The Name of the Wind* (New York: DAW Books, 2007), 1.

31. Lisa Mangum, *The Hourglass Door* (Salt Lake City: Shadow Mountain, 2009), 1.

Chapter 2: The Mathematics of Great Writing

1. *Toy Story 2*, directed by John Lasseter (1999; Burbank, CA: Disney/Pixar, 2010), DVD.

2. *Raiders of the Lost Ark*, directed by Steven Spielberg (1981; Los Angeles, CA: Paramount Pictures Home Entertainment, 2013), DVD.

3. Janice Hardy, "Oh, Woe Is Me: Strengthening Character Goals," Janice Hardy's Fiction University (blog), February 26, 2020, http://blog.janicehardy.com/2010/05/oh-woe-is-me.html.

4. Elizabeth Lowham, *Beauty Reborn* (Salt Lake City: Shadow Mountain, 2023), 1.

5. Mark Nichol, "How to Motivate Your Characters," Daily Writing Tips, accessed March 30, 2024, https://www.dailywritingtips.com/how-to-motivate-your-characters/.

6. Randy Ingermanson, "Goals and Motivations in Fiction Writing," Advanced Fiction Writing (blog), March 28, 2012, https://www.advancedfictionwriting.com/blog/2012/03/28/goals-and-motivations-in-fiction-writing/.

7. Vince Gilligan, dir., *Breaking Bad*. Season 1, episode 1, "Pilot." Aired January 20, 2008, on AMC.

8. Vince Gilligan, dir., *Breaking Bad*, Season 5, episode 16, "Felina." Aired September 29, 2013, on AMC.

9. See American Red Cross, "Responding to Emergencies: Comprehensive First Aid/CPR/AED" (PDF), 89, https://www.redcross.org/content/dam/redcross/training-services/course-fact-sheets/RTE-IM-Sample.pdf.

10. *Star Wars: A New Hope*, directed by George Lucas (1977; San Francisco, CA: Lucasfilm, 2019), DVD.

11. *The Empire Strikes Back*, directed by Irvin Kershner (1980; San Francisco, CA: Lucasfilm, 2019), DVD.

12. *Return of the Jedi*, directed by Richard Marquand (1983; San Francisco, CA: Lucasfilm, 2019), DVD.

13. *The Lord of the Rings: The Fellowship of the Ring*, directed by Peter Jackson (2001; Los Angeles, CA: New Line Home Entertainment, 2002), DVD.

14. *The Lord of the Rings: The Two Towers*, directed by Peter Jackson (2002; Los Angeles, CA: New Line Home Entertainment, 2003), DVD.

Chapter 3: Voice: Making Your Manuscript Sing

1. Stephen King, *The Dark Tower VII: The Dark Tower* (New York: Scribner, 2004), 817–18.

2. Gary Provost, *100 Ways to Improve Your Writing: Proven Professional Techniques for Writing with Style and Power, Revised and Updated* (New York: Berkley, 1972, 2019), 58.

3. Mangum, *The Hourglass Door*, 135.

4. "10 Steps to Finding Your Writing Voice," Jeff Goins, accessed March 30, 2024, http://goinswriter.com/writing-voice/.

5. See "10 Steps to Finding Your Writing Voice," http://goinswriter.com/writing-voice/.

6. Donald Maass, *Writing the Breakout Novel: Insider Advice for Taking Your Fiction to the Next Level* (New York: Writer's Digest Books, 2001), 195.

7. Patricia Lee Gauch, in *Writing for Children: The Report of the 1997 Highlights Foundation Writers Workshop at Chautauqua* (United States: Highlights Foundation, Incorporated, 1998), 13.

Chapter 4: How to Write an Ending—or a Sequel—That Doesn't Disappoint

1. Brandon Sanderson, writers conference.

2. *The Lord of the Rings: The Return of the King*, directed by Peter Jackson (2003; Los Angeles, CA: New Line Home Entertainment, 2004), DVD.

3. Eugenie Ross-Leming, quoted by Laura Prudom (@Lauraprudom), X, August 4, 2019, 5:49 p.m., https://twitter.com/lauraprudom/status/1158163063616393217.

4. Deborah Chester, *The Fantasy Fiction Formula* (Manchester, England: Manchester University Press, 2016), 88.

5. Tom Stoppard, *Rosencrantz and Guildenstern Are Dead* (New York: Grove Press, 1967), 79.

6. J. K. Rowling, *Harry Potter and the Sorcerer's Stone* (New York: Scholastic, 1998), 1.

7. *Serenity*, directed by Joss Whedon (2005; Universal City, CA: Universal Studios Home Entertainment, 2005), DVD.

8. See TV Tropes, s.v. "Bury Your Gays," accessed March 30, 2024, https://tvtropes.org/pmwiki/pmwiki.php/Main/BuryYourGays.

9. See TV Tropes, s.v. "Stuffed into the Fridge," accessed March 30, 2024, https://tvtropes.org/pmwiki/pmwiki.php/Main/StuffedIntoTheFridge.

10. Darren Mooney, "Black Widow's Death in Endgame Illustrates the Worst Type of Subversion," *The Escapist*, May 1, 2020, https://www.escapistmagazine.com/natasha-romanov-black-widow-death-avengers-endgame-worst-subversion/.

11. See Deborah Chester, *The Fantasy Fiction Formula* (Manchester, England: Manchester University Press, 2016), 257–70.

12. *Star Wars: A New Hope*, directed by George Lucas (1977; San Francisco, CA: Lucasfilm, 2019), DVD.

13. Wikipedia, s.v. "Hero's journey," last modified March 29, 2024, 10:17, https://en.wikipedia.org/wiki/Hero%27s_journey.

Notes

14. Tracy Hickman, personal conversation with author, March 21, 2024.

Chapter 5: Breaking through Writer's Block

1. Dennis Gaunt, personal letter to author, November 2010.

Chapter 7: A Fistful of Commas

1. *The Chicago Manual of Style, 17th Edition* (Chicago: University of Chicago Press, 2017), 7.81.
2. "I Can Remember (Bread, Milk, Butter)," Jim Simon, dir, *Sesame Street*, Season 4, episode 8. Aired November 22, 1972, on PBS.
3. David Nutter, dir., *Supernatural*, Season 1, episode 1, "Pilot." Aired September 13, 2005, on WB.
4. Phil Sgriccia, dir., *Supernatural*, Season 8, episode 23, "Sacrifice." Aired May 15, 2013, on CW.
5. Brandon Mull, *The Candy Shop War: Carnival Quest* (Salt Lake City: Shadow Mountain, 2023), 350.

Chapter 9: Query Letters and Pitching

1. Back cover copy. Sarah M. Eden, *The Queen and the Knave* (Salt Lake City: Shadow Mountain, 2023).
2. Jacket copy. McCall Hoyle, *Stella* (Salt Lake City: Shadow Mountain, 2021).
3. Jacket copy. Michaelbrent Collings, *Grimmworld: The Witch in the Woods* (Salt Lake City: Shadow Mountain, 2024).
4. See Wikipedia, s.v. "List of Writing Genres," last modified March 1, 2024, 07:21, https://en.wikipedia.org/wiki/List_of_writing_genres.

Chapter 10: Quit. But If You Can't . . .

1. Tracy Hickman, personal conversation with author, March 21, 2024.
2. Charles Beeson, dir., *Supernatural*, Season 2, episode 16, "Roadkill." Aired March 15, 2007, on CW.
3. Mary Oliver, "The Summer Day," in *New and Selected Poems, Volume One, Revised Edition* (Boston: Beacon Press, 1992), 94.

About the Author

Lisa Mangum has worked in publishing for more than twenty-five years. She has been the managing editor for Shadow Mountain since 2014 and has worked with several award winning and *New York Times* best-selling authors.

Lisa is also the author of four national best-selling YA novels (The Hourglass Door trilogy and *After Hello*), several short stories and novellas, and a nonfiction book about the craft of writing based on the TV show *Supernatural*.

She regularly teaches at writing conferences across the country as well as hosts a writing weekend twice a year in Capitol Reef National Park. She lives in Taylorsville, Utah, with her husband, Tracy.

Facebook: Lisa Mangum
Instagram: @authorlisamangum
X: @LisaMangum